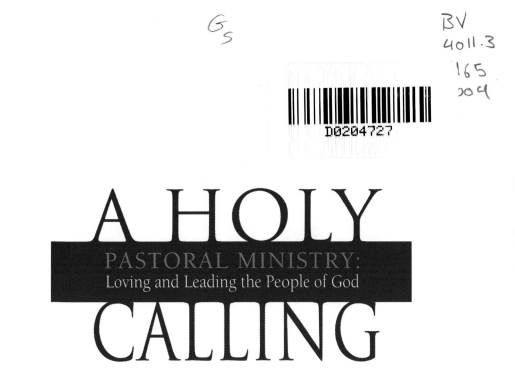

A HOLY

PASTORAL MINISTRY:
Loving and Leading the People of God

CALLING

A HOLY

PASTORAL MINISTRY:
Loving and Leading the People of God

CALLING

Compiled by

NEIL B. WISEMAN

and

CHARLES E. ZINK

Beacon Hill Press of Kansas City
Kansas City, Missouri

Copyright 2004
by Beacon Hill Press of Kansas City

ISBN 083-412-1425
Printed in the United States of America

Cover Design: Ted Ferguson

Bible Credits

Library of Congress Cataloging-in-Publication Data

A holy calling : pastoral ministry : loving and leading the people of God / Neil B. Wiseman and Charles E. Zink.
   p. cm.
   "A Palcon resource book for Nazarene ministers, 2004."
   ISBN 0-8341-2142-5 (pbk.)
   1. Pastoral theology. 2. Clergy—Office. I. Wiseman, Neil B. II. Zink, Charles E.

   BV4011.3.H65 2004
   253'.088'28799—dc22

               2004003073

CONTENTS

FOREWORD

Challenge of Our Mission

Dear Sisters and Brothers,

Please allow me to express my gratitude for your faithfulness to this important calling of shepherding believers in the Church of the Nazarene. Your ministry is vital to the redemptive work of the Kingdom, both in your local community and in our particular branch of Christ's Body. Without you and your partners in ministry, both clergy and laity, all efforts to maintain our heritage, to uphold our core values, and to carry out our mission would be in vain. I am optimistic about the future of the Church of the Nazarene, primarily because of the quality of my colleagues in ministry. God has blessed and gifted His Church by calling you to lead her.

As you peruse these three volumes prepared for PALCON 2004, I hope you will conclude as I have, that the subjects they address are vital to our ministry in the Church of the Nazarene. The degree of your faithfulness and mine to our preaching task, to our role as shepherds, and to our doctrine of holiness, will have a direct effect on the extent to which current and future generations will identify and distinguish themselves as a Missional, Christian, Holiness people.

Let us covenant together that the labors of these authors, whose ministries were and are so Spirit-filled, will not fall to the ground. Let us pray for guidance and inspiration from the Holy Spirit as we read their words, absorb their passion, and proceed as the inheritors of their spiritual legacy. May you find yourself refreshed, stimulated, and moved to action by what you read in these pages.

In His Peace,
Charles E. Zink
Director, Clergy Development

PREFACE

PASTORAL MINISTRY—SERVING CHRIST AT THE FRONT LINES

PASTOR—what a beautiful, holy word that describes the tender ties between the people of God and the shepherd of their souls.

Being a pastor—what a humbling promise of partnership with Omnipotence.

Being a pastor—what an awesome assignment when the accumulated meaning of the biblical metaphors concerning ministry are considered like farmer, soldier, athlete, servant of God, overseer, preacher of righteousness, and steward of grace.

This book is an anthology of important writings about pastoral ministry from several generations of Nazarene leaders. It clearly shows that from her beginnings at Pilot Point in 1908, the Church of the Nazarene has considered pastors to be the pivotal person in the work of every church.

The combined faithfulness of pastors across Nazarene history squares with scriptural directives. Our forefathers and foremothers had lofty and inspiring views of pastoral ministry, which they practiced and passed to oncoming generations, including us. If you are a Nazarene pastor, stand tall. You are among the most notable of all Nazarene leaders.

Read this book with squared shoulders and bowed hearts. Those who have gone before us in pastoral ministry served their generations well. Our call is to do as well in ours. And we will.

As founding director of the first PALCON in 1976-77, it gives me indescribable satisfaction to be involved in PALCON 2004. Part of my responsibility for this great PALCON series was selecting and editing these chapters on pastoral ministry.

Some of this material is relatively new, and other chapters are part of Nazarene history. (They have been edited only slightly, and therefore retain the writers' original work, in some cases complete with dated references and non-gender-inclusive language.)

My joy is full and my heart filled with gratitude for the accumulated impact the various PALCONs have had on our church. And I am glad to be a small part of PALCON 2004.

—Neil B. Wiseman

1

MISSIONAL MINISTERS FOR THESE TIMES

Jerry D. Porter

AROUND THE WORLD many heroic Great Commandment-Great Commission ministers are leading the Church of the Nazarene from entrenchment to outreach and from complacency to passion. They are leading us away from deadly maintenance to all-out missional effectiveness.

As we shall see, missional ministers in our church have four characteristics very much like the characteristics of leaders in the New Testament church. These missional ministers are evangelistic, compassionate, inclusive, and they reproduce themselves and their churches.

These characteristics echo the core values of our beloved church. The core values are (1) we are a Christian people; (2) we are a holiness people; (3) we are a missional people.

Travel with me to visit an exciting New Testament church where a missional minister serves as pastor, one nicknamed Barnabas. "In the church at Antioch there were prophets and teachers: Barnabas, Simeon . . . , Lucius . . . , Manaen . . . and Saul" (Acts 13:1).[1]

Who is this pastor-teacher, Barnabas?

How did he become this missional pastor of Antioch First Church?

Luke describes him as "a good man, full of the Holy Spirit and faith" (Acts 11:24).

As we study the missional characteristics of this godly leader in greater depth, we must underscore the fact that the first two core values of our Nazarene faith community are very evident in Barnabas:

1. WE ARE A CHRISTIAN PEOPLE.
2. WE ARE A HOLINESS PEOPLE.

Before we go off to win the world to Jesus we must *be* Jesus people. This New Testament pastor was a radically obedient disciple of Christ. He was a Holy Spirit-filled leader. What does 21st-century holiness look like? Holiness is Christlikeness—persons of genuine personal integrity. And that Christlikeness showed in Barnabas.

Barnabas was a living testimony of the cleansing and empowering fullness of the blessed Holy Spirit.

Barnabas was a trusted leader in the Jerusalem New Testament church. He was probably one of the 500 who witnessed the resurrection of our Lord and was likely among the 120 in the Upper Room on Pentecost Sunday. The Spirit's wind empowered these Christ-disciples to be bold witnesses, God's fire purified their hearts by faith, and the Gentile languages they spoke called them to be missionaries to reach all people everywhere.

Before we embrace the Barnabas missional mandate, by the grace of God, we must be Christlike, Spirit-filled disciples.

Our third core value is that *we are a missional people.* To be missional means we embrace Christ's mission. The Lord's mission is to draw everyone to the Kingdom. As individuals and as a global church we passionately commit ourselves to lift up Christ and call people everywhere to repentance and to new life.

A MISSIONAL MINISTER IS ENTHUSIASTICALLY EVANGELISTIC

How did Barnabas come to this church? Antioch First Church was an innovative, thriving fellowship. After Stephen's martyrdom many Jewish Christians migrated north to Antioch, a sports-crazed, chariot-racing city dedicated to the immoral worship of the goddess Daphne. Antioch was an important city of the Roman Empire, third only to Rome and Alexandria. In this setting the new Christians evangelized the Jewish residents.

OUR CREATIVE GOD CONSTANTLY SURPRISES US WITH NEW FORMS AND STRATEGIES TO ACCOMPLISH THE DIVINE MISSION.

Certain Jews from Cyprus and Cyrene, however, evangelized heathen Greeks, much to the shock of the general church. Leaders in Jerusalem sent Barnabas, a Levite who was fluent in Greek, to Antioch to investigate this unauthorized, innovative evangelism.

Are you surprised when the Lord God changes the methods? From New Testament times until now, the church has struggled with methods. In fact a change in methodology can divide the church quicker than issues of doctrine or holy living.

God is the same yesterday, today, and forever, but throughout the centuries, our creative God constantly surprises us with new forms and strategies to accomplish the divine mission. The message does not change, but new methods allow us to address our rapidly changing mission fields.

When Barnabas arrived in Antioch he celebrated the inclusion of these Greek Christians and stayed on to become the lead pastor. He focused on holistic evangelism, nurturing and discipling the new believers.

He understood, as we must understand, that our Lord's commission is much more than making converts. The mandate to Barnabas and to us is to *make Christlike disciples.* It was in Antioch that the followers of Jesus Christ were first called Christians. Some suggest that this was yet another inspiration of the pastoral team, naming the believers "little Christs." Some thought it mocked them, but the new name actually energized them to become radically more like the Christ.

In the midst of their enthusiastic evangelism in Antioch, Luke portrays what may have been a twice-a-week prayer and fasting service. "The Holy Spirit said, 'Set apart for me Barnabas and Saul for the work to which I have called them.' So after they had fasted and prayed, they placed their hands on them and sent them off" (Acts 13:2-3).

Without hesitation the church sent these pastors on an evangelistic missionary voyage. These were their most experienced, capable leaders and they went out to start churches.

We tend to find a multitude of reasons why the Lord should not send our best to the next town or to another mission field. "Lord, we can't survive without Barnabas and Paul!" Antioch First, however, was so passionate about reaching the lost and obeying the

> **"ALWAYS LOOK A RIOT IN THE FACE."**

Lord that they immediately sent these missional pastors on their way. The Word records that many persons embraced faith in Christ in the various cities where they proclaimed the message of Jesus, the Hope.

The abandon and commitment of Barnabas and Paul to their evangelistic mandate is obvious. In Lystra, "Some Jews came from Antioch and Iconium and won the crowd over. They stoned Paul and dragged him outside the city, thinking he was dead. But after the disciples had gathered around him, he got up and went back into the city" (4:19-20).

Paul was left for dead. The Lord's healing grace gave him strength to get up, and what did he do? Barnabas helped Paul walk right back into Lystra! John Wesley taught, "Always look a riot in the face." Today we need a double portion of their courageous passion to reach lost people.

In our day we are witnessing the Lord drawing multitudes unto himself. One-third of the world's population call themselves Christians.

In 1950 there were no recorded Christians in Nepal, and today there are over 300,000.

When the Communist revolution swept across China, there were 1 million Christians. Today there are more Christians in China than any other nation of the world, over 100 million!

In 1960 3 percent of the world's population were evangelical Christians. Today 11 percent embrace faith in Jesus Christ as their personal Savior.

Over the nearly 100 years of history of our beloved church, we celebrate the rich diversity of 1.54 million Nazarenes in 13,000 congregations in nearly 150 world areas. During the past 10 years 900,000 new Nazarenes joined our global church family. Each week during the 1997—2001 quadrennium 1,800 persons joined our fellowship and 13 new churches were launched. This past year through the Church of the Nazarene JESUS Film ministry, one new person embraced faith in our Lord every minute of every hour of every day.

WE MUST MOVE COURAGEOUSLY TO MULTIPLICATION STRATEGIES THAT WILL ALLOW US TO REACH THIS GENERATION FOR THE KINGDOM.

The challenge we face is overwhelming. The world population did not reach 1 billion until 1804. It reached 6 billion by 1999. Even as the Christian Church grows, there are more lost people every year. During the 20th century that number jumped from 1.2 billion to a staggering 4 billion lost persons.

Each time we gather for a 90-minute service, more than 12,000 people pass into eternity. Two-thirds of them die without Christ!

How shall we respond? Our Lord wants more from us than a fruitless, ineffective status quo. His commission is clear. We must move courageously to multiplication strategies that will allow us to reach this generation for the Kingdom.

Though our Christian Holiness Missional denomination is growing faster than ever, reaching more persons than ever, our percentage growth is declining.

Check our record during the 1989-93 quadrennium: each 6 members brought 1 new Nazarene each year. From 1993 to 1997 it took 8 to win 1. From 1997 to 2001 it took nearly 10 Nazarenes to win 1 new member per year.

A similar trend is emerging in church planting. From 1989 to 1993 it took 7 active congregations to begin 1 new church per year. During the next quadrennium each 8 churches started 1 new community of faith. From 1997 to 2001 it took 13 churches to launch 1 new congregation per year.

By God's grace we must and we will turn this around. Our church family yearns for each one to reach one, and each church to launch one!

As we move toward our denomination's centennial celebration in 2008, we pray our global fellowship will embrace anew the mission of our church to make Christlike disciples in all nations.

The denominational missional faith projections are to receive 1 million new Nazarenes in eight years (2000-2008), report 2 million persons in attendance and membership by 2008, with 1 million in weekly Bible study classes. Effective missional pastors are enthusiastic evangelists who empower and mobilize the laity in contagious Christian outreach.

A MISSIONAL MINISTER IS KNOWN FOR COMPASSIONATE JUSTICE

Luke first introduces us to this generous man named Barnabas, "Joseph, a Levite from Cyprus, whom the apostles called Barnabas (which means Son of

Encouragement), sold a field he owned and brought the money and put it at the apostles' feet" (Acts 4:36-37).

Barnabas sought no fanfare but created quite a stir with his donation. The Levites, as a tribe, had no land, but individual Levites could own personal property. In radical, transparent generosity he responded to the need and spontaneously gave what he had. The result was great enthusiasm throughout the whole congregation and community. Ananias and Saphira wanted to be honored in the same way but were not genuinely compassionate. They were play-acting, pretending to identify with the needy but simply seeking church popularity. Their hypocrisy cost them dearly, as the church's youth group buried them the very day they made their spectacular, public compassionate ministry donation!

This same generous Barnabas, a few years later, took a disaster relief love offering from Antioch First Church to the mother church in Jerusalem. Historian Josephus speaks of a terrible famine in Judea in the fourth year of the reign of the Roman Emperor Claudius. It was probably this devastating drought that stirred genuine compassion in the heart of Pastor Barnabas and the Antioch church.

A while ago my wife and I had a couple of days of rest in Toronto between Canadian assemblies. Following a lovely meal, as we were walking back to the hotel she was agonizing over the street people. She reminded me of the street children in Guatemala and the homeless in Baltimore whom we had helped. She insisted that we had to help at least one person that night.

A few minutes later Ken asked me for some change. I invited him to come into a pizza shop. This immigrant from Scotland said he was suffering from epilepsy and could no longer drive tractor trailers. He gratefully received the food, a gospel tract, and our gentle witness about God's love for him.

Sometimes we get overwhelmed by the immense needs and our limited resources. We cannot feed the whole world, but we can feed one. We cannot sponsor all the children—sponsor one. We cannot address every injustice—address one. We cannot care for all the orphans and widows—help one. I relearned a Barnabas lesson in Toronto that night.

This selfish, greedy, materialistic world would squeeze us into its mold. In recent years compassion evangelism has allowed us to enter more than 20 new mission fields. This Barnabas incarnational outreach may well be the most effective, and in some cases, the only evangelism tool God has given us. Mother Teresa said it so well:

> Riches, both material and spiritual, can choke you if you do not use them fairly. For not even God can put anything in a heart that is already full. One day there springs up the desire for money and for all that money can provide—the superfluous, luxury in eating, luxury in dressing, trifles. Needs increase because one thing calls for another. The result is uncontrol-

lable dissatisfaction. Let us remain as empty as possible so that God can fill us up.

With all the passion of her selfless lifestyle, Mother Teresa continues:

> The poor in the slums are without Jesus and we have the privilege of entering their homes . . . To go to the slums merely for the sake of going will not be enough to draw them to Jesus. If we are preoccupied with ourselves and our own affairs, we will not be able to live up to this ideal . . . The gospels remind us that Jesus, before He taught the people, felt compassion for the multitudes that followed after Him . . . He gave them food to eat until they couldn't eat anymore, and twelve basketfuls were left over. Then He taught them. Only then did He tell them the Good News.

She continues:

> Jesus gives me the opportunity to feed Him by feeding those who are hungry, to clothe Him by clothing those who are naked, to heal Him by caring for those who are sick, and to offer Him shelter by housing those who are homeless and unwanted.[2]

A MISSIONAL MINISTER IS MULTICULTURALLY AND GENDER INCLUSIVE

Barnabas was a global Christian. As we said earlier, he was fluent in Greek and held in high regard in the Jerusalem church. He was their emissary to investigate this radical new evangelistic approach. Nameless Jewish pioneers from Africa and Cyprus broke through the third and final barrier to allow the Christian faith to become global.

First, layperson Philip led a mighty revival among Samaritans. Then Peter had his strange dietary vision and witnessed the first Pentecost among God-fearing Gentiles. Then, stage three, these laypersons offered the Good News, not to Gentile followers of Jehovah, but to heathen Greeks.

It is not always easy for us to move from our racial prejudice to become multiculturally inclusive. These prejudices are embedded in our cultures and we pick them up as children. We are not guilty of racial sin until we recognize our prejudice and choose to do nothing about it.

Shortly after Barnabas and Paul's first missionary journey, Christians from Judea visited Antioch First Church and insisted that if the Gentiles were not circumcised, they could not be saved. "This brought Paul and Barnabas into sharp dispute and debate with them. So Paul and Barnabas were appointed, along with some other believers, to go up to Jerusalem to see the apostles and elders about this question" (Acts 15:2). Sharp, honest debate among believers is one of the ways God's Spirit guides His Church.

In Jerusalem, "The whole assembly became silent as they listened to Barnabas and Paul telling about the miraculous signs and wonders God had done among the Gentiles through them" (v. 12). Inclusive leaders, like Barnabas and

Paul, are a great gift to the church. They open our eyes to our prejudice, calling us to shatter the national, racial, and gender distinctions that would separate us from one another.

In his letter to the Galatians, Paul speaks of this historic general church meeting. "James, Peter, and John . . . gave me and Barnabas the right hand of fellowship. . . . They agreed that we should go to the Gentiles, and they to the Jews" (Gal. 2:9).

THE SIGN OVER EACH NAZARENE CHURCH ENTRANCE READS: "EVERYONE IS WELCOME HERE."

The gospel comes to us wrapped in the swaddling clothes of our culture. We focus our missionary work on a given people group without apology. At the same time every community of faith, be it Jewish, Greek, Haitian, Irish, Korean, or Texan, must be inclusive. The sign over each Nazarene church entrance reads: "Everyone is welcome here."

Paul continues in his Galatian letter to tell of General Superintendent Peter's visit to Antioch First Church. He was joyously sharing in a love feast with the Greek believers, until some scowling Jerusalem Christians arrived. Abruptly Peter and Barnabas rejected the Greek believers and started hanging out with the Jews!

It is tragic when, without thinking, we discriminate between persons because of their nationality, class, gender, color, wealth, language, or education. Peter and Barnabas had to humble themselves and apologize for their cowardly and insensitive treatment of the Greeks.

Our church faces challenging cultural and national obstacles to being a truly inclusive global church. Our personal unwillingness to admit our prejudice may be the greatest challenge. When we act in a biased way, we must humble ourselves and allow Christ to cleanse us by His Spirit. At the foot of the Cross there are no favored races, no preferred nations, no male nor female, no superior persons. We are all equals as brothers and sisters in Christ.

A MISSIONAL MINISTER REPRODUCES NEW PASTORS AND NEW CONGREGATIONS

Barnabas was not only evangelistic, compassionate, and inclusive but also very effective in launching new communities of faith and reproducing himself in new workers for these churches. Everywhere this missionary team went they organized churches, "Paul and Barnabas appointed elders for them in each church and, with prayer and fasting, committed them to the Lord" (Acts 14:23).

Can we evangelize the lost without planting churches? I don't think so. It never occurred to Barnabas and Paul that the Christian faith could be lived in isolation. By its very nature our Kingdom life is experienced in community. Faith without fellowship is dead. John Wesley reminds us that "no one ever went to heaven alone."

EVERY ONE OF OUR CHURCHES WAS FIRST A VISION ON SOMEONE'S HEART WHILE OTHERS ARGUED AGAINST THE CHURCH PLANT.

The 21st-century missional minister is committed to reproducing healthy new communities of faith. Church planting is one of the most effective ways to reach lost people. Missional pastors do not ask, "What is in it for me?" but rather, "What is best for the lost and for the Kingdom?"

Our Nazarene passion is to launch new churches in each community and people group around the world. Every one of our churches was first a vision on someone's heart while others argued against the church plant. When I served as the Mexico-Central America regional director, I compiled a list of 22 excellent excuses why "we cannot launch a daughter church; not here, not this way, not us, not yet." Our love for Christ and for the lost melts away these nearsighted obstacles as we sacrificially obey the call to launch these "centers of holy fire."

To plant these congregations, missional ministers reproduce themselves in the next generation of ministers. It was Barnabas who empowered new convert Saul and introduced him to the fearful Jerusalem church. Barnabas took the risk and believed in this church persecutor-turned-evangelist. After becoming pastor at Antioch, Barnabas again sought Saul, to deploy him as associate pastor for outreach and evangelism. For a whole year Barnabas discipled Saul and three other diverse associate pastors.

When the Holy Spirit moved Barnabas and Saul from the local church to a regional church-planting ministry, Barnabas was the apparent leader. In Lystra, where the Lord performed a majestic miracle, the people began to worship Barnabas and Paul as gods. They called Barnabas Jupiter, the supreme god of the heathens; and Paul they called Mercury, the god of eloquence. Some scholars suggest that Barnabas was the older, noble, larger leader and Paul was the younger, smaller, eloquent preacher.

Luke mentions Barnabas before Paul every time until Acts 13:13. From then on the order is reversed. The associate pastor had become the missionary leader. The elder, more experienced veteran passed the baton to the next-generation pastor. Missional pastors joyfully reproduce themselves in the next generation of church planters and pastors.

Shortly after the Jerusalem General Board meeting, Paul suggested that it would be great to visit the churches they had organized. Barnabas agreed and recommended they again recruit John Mark. Paul had no interest in Mark, who abandoned them on their first trip. "They had such a sharp disagreement that they parted company" (Acts 15:39).

Both Barnabas and Paul were sanctified stubborn. They honored and loved each other in Christ, but they did not agree on strategy. Barnabas would not embark without his younger cousin, John Mark. Paul did not want a flaky, immature missionary on the team. Finally, I believe by divine provocation, they became two missionary teams. Paul took Luke, Silas, and Timothy, the first Gentile missionary. Barnabas headed for his Mediterranean home in Cyprus with Mark.

Luke says nothing more about missional Pastor Barnabas. But that is not the end of the story. Barnabas encouraged and empowered a young leader. Mark went on to write the earliest Gospel a couple of decades after the resurrection of our Lord. The apostle Peter speaks of Mark as his "son" and may have even dictated the Gospel that Mark wrote. Later Mark ministered with Paul on his last missionary voyage, and in Paul's prison Epistle to the Colossians, he conveys greetings from John Mark, his faithful companion.

The "Barnabas pattern" is a low-profile reproducing pastor. It is amazing what can be done for God if we do what is right and don't care who gets the credit. Our church needs a host of visionary humble ministers who primarily seek the advance of the Lord's kingdom rather than their own kingdom. The testimony of our faithfulness to God's call is that we are Christlike missional pastors wherever we serve. In fact, it is through innovative, grassroots pastors that we discover the 21st-century methods God will bless and use.

Barnabas nurtured Paul and then worked himself out of a job. He developed Mark and then Peter and Paul recruited this associate pastor for their ministry teams, while Barnabas quietly disappeared from recorded church history.

What would have happened in the life of the church if Barnabas had not developed and empowered Paul and John Mark?

The future of the Church of the Nazarene lies primarily in the hands of faithful, creative, often unheralded, empowering, missional pastors. These ministers are not primarily seeking position and authority; they are first and foremost Kingdom driven. They find their greatest joy, not in their own ministerial success, but in the victories of their disciples.

Having capable, Spirit-motivated pastoral candidates assures us success in multiplying congregations. Without these workers our church planting strategies are a royal waste of time. The vision of the Church of the Nazarene to launch thousands of new communities of faith calls for a collective, denomination-wide crusade. We must preach about God's call, nurture the call, and help these candidates prepare for Christian service.

Our global faith projection is to report 18,000 churches by 2008. Is this challenge too small? Would the Lord want His Church to move from addition to multiplication?

If each Nazarene congregation would launch a new faith community every three or four years, we would celebrate our centennial with nearly 50,000 church fellowships.

If each Nazarene would bring one person to Christ and the church every three or four years, we would report over 5 million Nazarenes by 2008 rather than 2 million.

In the book *The Tipping Point,* the author speaks of social epidemics that spread like a virus, introducing rapid change to a given community or society. He illustrates the power of exponential change. If we add a sheet of paper 50 times, we simply have a stack of 50 sheets of paper. What happens if we fold a sheet of paper in half 50 times, each time doubling the number of sheets?

THE NEW TESTAMENT CHURCH MOVED FROM GRADUAL TO EXPONENTIAL GROWTH AND SO MUST WE.

Several factors come together to tip the scales in favor of dramatic, rapid change rather than slow, gradual change. The mission of our church is to make Christlike disciples in all nations. Our global church yearns to reach as many persons, as effectively as possible, as quickly as possible. Slow, healthy growth is not better than rapid, healthy growth. Folding the paper in half 50 times would create a tower of paper equal to the distance from the earth to the sun!

The New Testament Church moved from gradual to exponential growth and so must we, by the grace of God. With modern technology and with sharpened, effective evangelism, discipleship, and church planting tools we must move to multiplication growth, to the glory of God.

Dr. Louise Chapman, a powerful Nazarene missions leader, said, "Aim high, set challenging goals, don't settle for too little."

Missional Pastor Barnabas was evangelistic, compassionate, inclusive, and reproducing new pastors and churches. May we embrace anew the call to be truly missional pastors. You are God's gift to a lost world.

Your church and your world desperately need you.

---

1. All Scripture references in this chapter are taken from the *Holy Bible, New International Version®* (NIV®). Copyright © 1973, 1978, 1984 by International Bible Society. Used by permission of Zondervan Publishing House. All rights reserved.

2. Mother Teresa, *No Greater Love* (Novato, Calif.: New World Library, 1997), 95, 99-100.

Adapted from a plenary message to the General Assembly of the Church of the Nazarene, in Indianapolis, Indiana, August 2001.

A Prayer:

O God,

wake us up to Jesus.

Give us His passion for prayer

and His passion for people.

May our needs drive us to Thee

and the needs of others

drive us to them.

Amen.

—E. Stanley Jones

From *Sayings of E. Stanley Jones,* ed. Whitney J. Dough (Franklin, Tenn.: Providence House Publishers, 1994), 106.

2

NAZARENE: OUR FAMILY NAME PROVIDES UNIQUE FOCUS FOR MINISTRY

John C. Bowling

HE WILL BE CALLED *a Nazarene* (Matt. 2:23).[1]

He went to Nazareth, where he had been brought up, and on the Sabbath day he went into the synagogue, as was his custom. And he stood up to read. The scroll of the prophet Isaiah was handed to him. Unrolling it, he found the place where it is written:
"The Spirit of the Lord is on me,
   because he has anointed me
   to preach good news to the poor.
He has sent me to proclaim freedom for the prisoners
   and recovery of sight for the blind,
to release the oppressed,
   to proclaim the year of the Lord's favor."
Then he rolled up the scroll, gave it back to the attendant and sat down. The eyes of everyone in the synagogue were fastened on him, and he began by saying to them, "Today this scripture is fulfilled in your hearing" (Luke 4:16-21).

Imagine someone deciding to build a huge factory: buying the land, hiring an architect and builder, arranging the financing, bringing the project to completion, assembling all the machinery, hiring a work force, and then sitting down to ask, "What product should we manufacture? What's supposed to go out of those double doors of the shipping department and on to semitrailers and railroad cars? Why did we build this factory?"

Or picture someone getting a group of world-class athletes together. Entering into contracts to pay them huge sums of money, hiring coaches and assistants, securing the lease on a great stadium, and then saying, "Let's see now, what kind of sport should we play?"

Or think about a group of individuals securing property, building build-

MISSION DRIVES, NOT FOLLOWS A GREAT WORK.

ings, and creating a beautiful campus. Providing all kinds of classroom equipment and teaching aids in the sciences, in the humanities, in the arts, enlisting a well-trained and gifted faculty and then when it is all in place asking, "Now what was it we were going to do?"

No one starts a work and moves then to mission. Folks start with a mission and then shape the work and use the resources to accomplish the mission. Mission drives, not follows a great work.

A problem, however, sometimes develops as people join the work in progress and begin to function as part of the group, without ever really owning the dream or envisioning the vision.

If you were hired on in the midst of building the factory, for example, that might be all you would do at first. It could be easy for you, under those circumstances, to become convinced that the work of that particular business is the building and the maintenance of the factory itself. It is dangerously easy for a means to become an end in itself.

It can be that way in our work as well. We have joined the Church with the work already in progress. And, as leaders, we are called upon to spend so much of our time and energy building and managing the organization that those endeavors become ends in themselves. So opportunities to focus on our continuing mission are very helpful.

We must ask the right questions: "Why are we doing this? What is the reason for all of the effort and toil? What is our mission? Where will we be when we get to where we're going?"

No church, no institution within the church, can minister effectively once it loses sight of its mission; for most of the time in life, you get what you expect. For a believer, vision and faith are inseparably linked, for faith is the evidence of things not seen. Faith is vision and vision is seeing it long before it is.

If you can see great things for God,
you can attempt great things for God.
If you attempt great things for God,
you can realize great things for God.

Tell me your vision and I will tell you your future.

Growing churches, schools, and ministries expect and plan, in advance, to grow. Much of life is a self-fulfilling prophecy. And we all know of the pull upon institutions to shift from dreaming to drifting, from mission to maintenance. To counter this pull we must have moments of renewal.

I want us to consider two passages of Scripture—one by way of introduction, from Matt. 2, and then a second passage from Luke 4. In these two passages we find the person and the power for mission renewal.

First this single verse from Matt. 2:23, "And he went and lived in a town called Nazareth. So was fulfilled what was said through the prophets: 'He will be called a Nazarene.'"

We are all interested in names. We give our names when we meet, we sign our names when we write, and we pass our names on to our children. Many of you know the Vail family from ONU, NNU, and PLNU. Larry Vail is a member of our faculty, and not long ago as he and his wife were expecting another child they considered biblical names. I suggested Noah, but Larry told me that "Noah Vail" was not the kind of name they had in mind.

There is a pastor on our region with a family in his church that has four sons: Matthew, Mark, Luke, and Roy.

Names are part of us. They are more than just titles or "handles" or tags for the purpose of identification. Parents plan for months to choose the right name for their children, not long after birth the child embodies and begins to define that name.

You see, there is a difference between saying, "My name is John Bowling," and saying, "I am John Bowling." I am more than a name. I am, in fact, the person who defines, for good or ill, what that name means.

When I was growing up in western Ohio, I remember my father saying to me, "John, our family name is a good name. I expect you and your brother to live up to your name. This means you won't act like some of the other boys or talk like some others, or go, or do, as others. You are part of this family, and we have certain standards."

I didn't always uphold the family name, but I never forgot what he told me and I do feel a sense of obligation to my family because what I do, where I go, and how I live reflects on that good name.

I am suggesting that names have meaning in two dimensions: the objective and the subjective.

1. Objectively, certain ideas can be expressed in the name as it is given to you. Nationality and family heritage are qualities bestowed upon you and often revealed in your name.

The names O'Brien, O'Reilly, and Kelly say something objectively about the persons who bear those names. The names Rodriguez, Hernandez, and Gutierrez say something completely different. Olivet is located in the village of Bourbonnais, a French-Catholic community. So in our community you encounter names like Lebeau, LaVassuer, and Boudreau.

Other names speak objectively, not of nationality, but of family trades. The Millers ran the mill, the Coopers were barrel makers, the Smiths were smiths, the Potters were potters, and so on.

So names have a certain objective character, but in addition to that there is the subjective nature of names.

2. Subjective meanings are the ways in which *you* define the name you have. What does your name come to mean as you flesh it out across the years?

Jack Stone was just a name until I got to know him, until we shared times and feelings and experiences and I came to know who he was. A name is just a name until we know that individual's values and traits, until we observe actions and reactions.

So there are objective and subjective characteristics of a name. I want us to think about the qualities of a name given to Jesus. We find that name in the verse from Matt. 2, "He will be called a Nazarene."

I attended a Southern Baptist Seminary for my doctoral work, the largest seminary in the world. Some of the most rewarding experiences I had when I was there were times in chapel services when we would sing the hymn "My Savior's Love." I remember it happening two or three times. When the hymn was announced, I would get ready by putting a textbook or two on the floor in front of me. As we stood to sing with all my Baptist buddies around me—I would wait through the introduction and just as we started to sing, "I stand amazed in the presence of Jesus the Nazarene," I would step up on those books and stand a little bit taller and look down the row and smile at all my friends.

> JESUS CHRIST
> TOOK THAT NAME
> AND FLOODED IT
> WITH NEW MEANING.

I was proud to be identified with Jesus, the Nazarene.

Objectively however, that name, Nazarene, was not historically a complimentary name. This is hinted at in John 1 when Nathanael, upon hearing of Jesus from Philip, uttered that intriguing question, "Can anything good come out of Nazareth?"

You see, Nazareth was in Galilee and those in Judea looked upon all the inhabitants of Galilee with a certain amount of contempt, for the Galileans were less cultivated. They spoke with a ruder accent. They were, by geographic location, more easily exposed to the Gentiles. And this question of Nathanael was perhaps even more revealing, for Nathaneal was a Galilean himself. So even among the Galileans, Nazareth had a poor reputation. Even those who were looked down upon looked down upon Nazarenes.

Objectively this was not a complimentary name. Yet Jesus Christ took that name and flooded it with new meaning. Subjectively, the life, teachings, ministry, compassion, death, and resurrection of Jesus served to give the name Nazarene new meaning. So much so that thousands upon thousands of people travel the distance of the globe each year to visit Nazareth. The town is not that much different today than it ever was—except for the fact that He was there and His presence made all the difference.

Now each of us, in addition to our given names and our family names and our titles, bear another name: Nazarene. Where do we turn to define that name today?

OBJECTIVELY

A. We can certainly turn to our heritage as we seek to understand what it means to be a Nazarene.

As you know it was Dr. J. P. Widney, a medical doctor, a colleague of Dr. Bresee, who suggested the name Church of the Nazarene. On the day Bresee and Widney organized their church, Dr. Widney spoke using the words of Christ, "Follow me," as his text. In that message he explained the choice of the name for the church.

The name Nazarene had come to him one morning at daybreak after a night of prayer. It immediately seemed to symbolize the toiling, lowly mission of Christ. Widney declared: "The name which was used in derision of Him by His enemies, the name above all others which linked Him to the great struggling, sorrowing heart of the world was Nazarene. It is Jesus the Nazarene to whom the world in its misery and despair turns." The name Church of the Nazarene was born. Where do we look to define the name? We look to our heritage, and

B. We also look to our doctrine.

The purpose of the Church of the Nazarene was to spread scriptural holiness throughout the world, to promote and preserve the doctrine of entire sanctification whereby a person is cleansed by the presence of the Holy Spirit and made holy.

We sprang from the Holiness Movement. It was in the hearts of our founders to establish centers of holy fire in every community, thereby having a part in the renewing of the Church of Jesus Christ, so that we might "Christianize Christianity" as Bresee put it. This is not only our doctrine but also our distinctive doctrine.

So, objectively the Church of the Nazarene can be understood, at least in part, in terms of our heritage and doctrine.

But now let's move from the objective side to the subjective side. How is the Church of the Nazarene defined in me and in my local church, in my area of ministry?

> OUR MISSION IS TO BE FOUND IN THE LIFE OF THE PERSON WHOSE NAME WE BEAR.

Most of the people outside the church have little interest in our heritage or even our doctrine at first. People will show interest in the church as we show interest in them. I must then embody our heritage and our doctrine, in personal ways. Therefore our true identity is ultimately found not in our heritage alone, nor in our theology, per se—ultimately our meaning, our message, and our mission is to be found in the life of the person whose name we bear, for we are the Church of the Nazarene.

"Of" is a possessive or genitive preposition. That means it shows owner-ship. The Church owned (possessed) by the Nazarene.

- If we are not like Christ, we are not the Church.
- If our heritage does not lead us once more to Him, we've missed it.
- If our doctrine does not serve to introduce Him to a lost and dying world, we have lost our way.

Mission is renewed within me only as the relationship is renewed. It is not my plans or programs that finally make the difference—it is the person called the Nazarene.

His mission must be mirrored in our mission. Many voices around us would seek to dictate the character of the church. Scores of people outside the church want to tell me what the mission and values and priorities of Olivet ought to be—but I must listen for His voice above them all, if it is to be His school.

This brings us to the second passage of the evening, Luke 4:18-21.

Here Jesus the Nazarene has returned to Nazareth. On the Sabbath day, He makes His way to the synagogue. There He takes the scroll of Isaiah and turns to a messianic section and begins to read:

> The Spirit of the Lord is on me, because he has anointed me to preach good news to the poor. He has sent me to proclaim freedom for the prison-ers and recovery of sight for the blind, to release the oppressed, to proclaim the year of the Lord's favor. Then he rolled up the scroll, gave it back to the attendant and sat down. The eyes of everyone in the synagogue were fas-tened on him, and he began to speak to them, "Today this scripture is ful-filled in your hearing."

Here is the Nazarene defining His mission.

The passage begins with the phrase, "The Spirit of the Lord is on me, be-cause he has anointed me." What follows then must therefore be a Spirit-filled ministry. Just as the Spirit anointed Jesus for His ministry, so each of us and all of us and our various places of ministry within the church must also be anointed with His Spirit. Therein does our objective heritage and doctrine become for us a subjective experience of faith. I must be able to testify with our founders and with Christ, "The Spirit of the Lord is on me, because he has anointed me."

The anointing gives us power and confidence. Herein is the power for mis-sion renewal. The Spirit brings faith and hope and peace—all the fruit and gifts of the Spirit are ours as an enablement for ministry. This includes the gift of joy and certainly our work and worship should be a joyful labor of love.

We have come a long way from the "glory barn" days of Dr. Bresee, and I know that we can't live in the past or reproduce it exactly; but if the ministry and mission of the church is Spirit-anointed, it will be a joyful and attractive thing.

The anointing of the Spirit brings power and the very presence of God into our midst, and it ought to show in our spirit and in our fellowship as we give ourselves to the mission of Christ.

In describing His mission, Jesus begins where we all must begin, with the anointing of the Spirit. He then quickly speaks of preaching the good news, of proclaiming freedom from bondage, sight for the blind, and release for the oppressed. And we see in that mission our continuing mission—preaching, teaching, equipping, and enabling.

We exist to manifest the life and power of Jesus Christ in the fulfillment of the ministry given to Him by the Father. We are His body—we are His people, we bear His name. The world needs the Church today, maybe more than ever before, and the world needs the Church of the Nazarene.

> WE EXIST TO MANIFEST THE LIFE AND POWER OF JESUS CHRIST.

THE CHALLENGE BEFORE US

As we move steadily toward our church's 100th birthday, time is not our ally. Scholars have suggested there is a drift that effects all institutions in time, one that moves them from being mission-driven to maintenance-driven. Those who study such things imply that this institutional arthritis cannot be prevented; it is a natural part of the aging process. It can, at best, be only retarded.

I think they are right, except for one thing. That is the possibility of mission renewal. If the mission of an institution is clearly and pervasively renewed, reembraced, revived, there results a kind of new beginning and the cycle starts over.

The embers are ignited, the warmth returns, the light brightens, and fire begins to burn. Every time we, in the Church of the Nazarene, lift the name of Jesus the Nazarene our mission is renewed. Every sermon that calls us to entire sanctification fans the flame. Every leader whose model of service is Jesus alone embodies Bresee's and Widney's dream. The person is Jesus; the power is the anointing of His Spirit.

> THE EMBERS ARE IGNITED, THE WARMTH RETURNS, THE LIGHT BRIGHTENS, AND FIRE BEGINS TO BURN.

I am encouraged. I believe we are committed to seizing this moment in our history, with a boundless boldness to believe in and to embody the person of Christ and to continue His mission.

> *I stand amazed in the presence of Jesus the Nazarene,*
> *And wonder how He could love me, a sinner, condemned, unclean.*
> *How marvelous! How wonderful! And my song shall ever be:*
> *How marvelous, how wonderful, is my Savior's love for me!*

The Church of the Nazarene is moving on—with purpose and with power; and I am glad to be a part of it.

---

1. All Scripture references in this chapter are taken from the *Holy Bible, New International-al Version*® (NIV®). Copyright © 1973, 1978, 1984 by International Bible Society. Used by permission of Zondervan Publishing House. All rights reserved.

Adapted from an address to the Nazarene Leadership Conference in Nashville, February 15-17, 2003.

There is probably no joy

that a soul ever felt

that is superior

to that experienced by a human heart

in this process of the

fusing of the divine truth,

by the divine Spirit, and being

the avenue of its outpouring.

This is especially so

when it is for and given

unto a people

carried upon the heart

of the preacher,

where every joy and sorrow,

despair and hope,

are part of his own life.

—Phineas F. Bresee

From *The Quotable Bresee,* Harold Ivan Smith, compiler (Kansas City: Beacon Hill Press of Kansas City, 1983), 158-59.

3

WOMEN AND MEN SERVING TOGETHER IN MINISTRY: FROM RHETORIC TO REALITY

Janine T. Metcalf

"WELCOME, PASTOR! Welcome, Pastor!"

As we stepped out of the car to attend our new congregation's July 4th picnic, my husband and I were overwhelmed by the fanfare. Children ran to us with arms waving. Senior adults ambled closer with their canes and walkers. Young adults suspended their softball game to join the march and spontaneous cheer. "Pastor's here! Pastor's here!"

The many roles that have defined my life journey—wife, mother, professor, evangelist, staff minister, television reporter—converged the moment I was called "Pastor."

Ed smiled and said, "Pastor, I like the sound of that!"

I nodded and replied, "I do too."

Ironically, the call to serve El Cajon Church of the Nazarene almost did not happen. A week before the pastoral vote, a regular attendee mailed a six-page letter to each family denouncing women in church leadership. He chastised the church board for not heeding what he defined as the biblical prohibition of women in pastoral office. He warned members that calling a woman to preach and pastor would incur the wrath of God and jeopardize the church's future. Despite his fierce campaign, the church overwhelmingly voted to call me.

I am exceedingly thankful. Not just for me, not just for my congregation, but also for the sake of Christ-centered mutuality that should typify Christian churches everywhere. This congregation represents a small but steadily growing number of Nazarene churches willing to embrace our century-old polity of gender partnership in leadership ministry. How did a Southern California church family in a community strongly influenced by conservative views call a woman to be their shepherd? The call was probably the result of intentional education and affirmation from the district superintendent, consistent prayer to seek

God's guidance, courage to address dissension with grace, and an ultimate resolve to do what was biblically sound and morally right.

I long to see this pattern repeated by churches throughout our denomination. The fulfillment of a call to ministry by hundreds of women currently preparing for pastoral ministry depends on it. And the accomplishment God has in mind for them will be missed by the church.

THE OPPORTUNITY FOR WOMEN TO PREACH AND LEAD CONGREGATIONS GOES DEEP IN OUR NAZARENE ROOTS.

Encouraged by what appears to be more ministerial options and cultural changes that foster gender mutuality, impressive numbers of Nazarene women have entered the ordination track. Women constitute more than 50 percent of the religion majors at Northwest Nazarene University. Similarly, more than 40 percent of the students at Nazarene Theological Seminary are women. These seminarians are following the footsteps of our Nazarene foremothers, whose sacrifice and holy boldness helped shape the identity and mission of the Church of the Nazarene.

The opportunity for women to preach and lead congregations goes deep in our Nazarene roots. It was sanctioned as early as 1892 when the Central Evangelical Holiness Association, a parent body of the Church of the Nazarene, ordained Anna Hanscome, pastor of a holiness congregation in Malden, Massachusetts. She became one of the first women ordained in America. Three years later, charter members of the First Church of the Nazarene in Los Angeles included the following gender-inclusive statement in their 1895 incorporation papers, "We recognize the equal right of both men and women to all offices of the church, including the ministry."[1]

First Church founder Phineas Bresee contended that the Holy Spirit who dispensed gifts and graces to the first Christians, still equipped men and women to spread the gospel, regardless of gender. Moving beyond rhetoric, Bresee ordained Elsie Wallace in 1902. Wallace was the founding pastor of Spokane, Washington, First Church and the first woman to be appointed a Nazarene district superintendent in North America.[2] The following year, he ordained Lucy Knott, pastor of the Mateo Street Mission in Los Angeles.[3] Bresee acknowledged Knott's effectiveness in a tribute to his coworkers, "As a preacher and leader in the church," he said, "she has shown peculiar ability. The Lord has greatly blessed her work, giving her a constant tide of salvation among all classes, from little children to old people."[4]

Knott and Wallace were among many Nazarene matriarchs who stepped beyond cultural and ecclesiastical barriers to share the gospel. Other dynamic leaders include Rev. Mary Lee Cagle, who organized 18 churches in four southern states, and Rev. Lucia Carmen de Costa, who planted 17 churches in the provincial capitals of Argentina.[5]

Aside from pastoring, Nazarene women expressed their leadership gifts by helping to launch the denomination's foreign missionary work, youth work, social programs, and its first educational institution. The Pacific Bible School was organized in 1901 by three laywomen to train up Christian workers. In two years, the faculty consisted of five women and three men headed by a female principal.[6]

Within the Church of the Nazarene's first 30 years, more than 20 percent of our credentialed ministers were women. These matriarchs risked misunderstanding and, in some cases, their lives to heed God's call to preach and pastor. Their faithful obedience helped convert countless souls, and paved the way for future generations of women to reach their highest ministerial potential. Unfortunately, by the mid to late 1930s Nazarene women began to vanish from the rolls of pastors, evangelists, and ministerial students. Key reasons for their disappearance continue to plague today's church. Some of these include:

Disagreement over the controversial passages of Paul that would seem to prohibit women from speaking and leading in the church (1 Cor. 14:34-35; 1 Tim. 2:11-15). Certain conservative evangelical leaders contend these passages clearly affirm the principle of male headship in the home and church. However, before issuing a blanket prohibition against women preaching and leading in ministry, the church should take a closer look at the historical and literary context of these passages. Did Paul intend to generally limit ministry roles available to women, or was he addressing specific problems that most likely existed in Corinth and Ephesus? Do these verses support or contradict an overall tenor of Scripture that encourages every believer to use his or her spiritual gifts to help build the Body of Christ?

Discrimination against women throughout history. Male dominance and female subordination have characterized most cultures since the dawn of recorded history. In Christ's day, a woman in Palestine had the legal status of a slave or an animal. Only the husband had the right of divorce, and he could turn his wife out of the home for almost any reason of displeasure. C. S. Cowles elaborates:

> Jewish literature is full of expressions of joy over the birth of a son and sorrow over the birth of a daughter. The Genesis commentary called the "Rabbah," written by the Rabbis, describes women as "greedy, eavesdroppers, lazy, jealous, querulous, and garrulous." Rabbi Hillel, grandfather of Gamaliel, taught that wherever women gathered together there was much witchcraft. A good Pharisee prayed, "O God, I thank thee that thou didst not create me a Gentile, a dog, or a woman."[7]

Imagine the joy felt by Jewish and Gentile women when Jesus addressed them with dignity and allowed them to sit and listen to His teaching. Women who had been barred from the inner courts of the Temple and synagogue worship were encouraged to draw near and receive the truth. A few of those women who had served Christ and faithfully stood by to watch the Crucifixion were the first to receive and spread the good news of the Resurrection. Later, the Book of Acts and Paul's letters indicate that women such as Philip's daughters, Prisca and Phoebe, played key roles in spreading the salvation story (Acts 21:7-9; Rom. 16:1-5).

The right of women to continue to pass on the gospel, however, was later curtailed by influential Church Fathers. By the middle of the second century, Tertullian offered these principles regarding a woman's role in worship: "It is not permitted for a woman to speak in the church, nor is it permitted for her to teach, nor to baptize, nor to offer [the Eucharist], nor any claim for herself a share in any masculine function—not to mention any priestly office."[8]

This patriarchal stance was most likely adopted to help spread the gospel without causing additional social upheaval. It was also used to combat heresies, such as Gnosticism, that often supported women in ministry but also denied that Jesus was a real human being. Regardless of the reason, most women were prohibited from preaching and leadership positions in the Church for the next 1,700 years. It was not until the American holiness movement that any sustained challenge to sexual discrimination against women in the church was launched.

A backlash to the women's liberation movement of the 1960s and 1970s. Outspoken conservative evangelical leaders have blamed most of the ills afflicting families today on radical feminism that emerged in the last four decades. Feminists, who sought equal rights for women in the workplace, were blamed for encouraging women to seek educational and professional fulfillment outside of the home. Many conservatives deplored this movement toward financial and emotional independence, claiming that it undermined "traditional family values."

Is it fair, however, to link all or most of today's family pressures with "women's lib"? Is the woman the only parent responsible for maintaining a loving, nurturing environment for raising children? Is it possible to model before children a Christlike partnership in which husbands and wives share responsibilities according to their gifts and availability?

My parents modeled this kind of mutual servanthood. My father exemplified spiritual headship by respecting my mother, listening to her, affirming her efforts to grow, and serving her in any needed task including monotonous housework.

Lack of change agents preserves the status quo. Nazarene women ministers need advocates in church leadership who are informed and intentional in promoting mutuality. Cowles insists: "All God-called and Spirit-filled potential ministers are 'dead in the water' until someone in a position of authority recognizes their gifts, invites them to participate in increasingly responsible forms of ministry, supports them in times of challenge, and encourages them along the way."[9]

I thank God for several church leaders who have consistently affirmed God's call in my life. Unfortunately, I know several other women pastors and ministerial students who need spiritual mentors to pray them through the loneliness and numerous challenges of stepping into a male-dominated field. Tragically, some have left the Church of the Nazarene to pastor churches in denominations that have actively embraced their gifts, pursued, and placed them.

THE VOLATILE ISSUE OF ENDORSING WOMEN IN CHURCH LEADERSHIP WILL NOT BE SOLVED BY FORCE OR NEGLECT.

How can our denomination prevent the further exodus of anointed women leaders? Not by mandate! Henri Nouwen wisely observed: "Nobody can force the soul of a community. The only possibility open is to create conditions in which the community can freely develop and discover the ways that lead to redemption."[10]

Nazarene leaders, numbed by the complexities of gender discrimination, should seriously consider this precept. The volatile issue of endorsing women in church leadership will not be solved by force or neglect. Our most viable recourse is to help congregations examine the effects of gender hierarchy versus mutuality in ministry, and provide strategies for change.

Here are four personal proposals to end the stalemate:

Pray for wisdom and courage. Sexism in and outside the Church is far more than a social ill. It is a spiritual battle that continues to divide believers and undermine the message and witness of congregations. Thus prayer must envelop all our endeavors to promote mutuality. Gretchen Gaebelein Hull contends: "In all warfare, an effective strategy is to divide and conquer, and Satan will use any method possible to divide believers and trick them into competing with one another for kingdom posts."[11]

May we prayerfully seek God's guidance to build healthy relationships between men and women in our homes and churches, to cherish and celebrate our God-given differences. May Christ's love prompt male pastors to invite women into the conversation, to hear them and value their input. May Christ's love free women pastors from resentment and self-pity, so that we may channel our attention to the gospel mission. This battle will require an ongoing commitment to pray that God's kingdom reign will prevail, that strongholds of prejudice will come down, and that the church will become the model of reconciliation God intends it to be.

Post our apologetic. The 2001 amendment to the *Manual* regarding women in ministry is an important tool to defend mutuality.[12] To expand its exposure, the statement could be posted on our denomination's official web site. This would provide easier access to our official stance. It also allows for expansion of the rationale. While Bible verses are sprinkled throughout the apologetic, more information is required to reveal their meaning and relevance. Thus, the statement could provide "links" to further explanations of each passage cited. Nazarenes need to know why Paul's restrictive passages should be examined in their literary and cultural context. By clicking on the highlighted 1 Cor. 14:33-34, they would receive an in-depth exegesis of the passage prepared by a Nazarene biblical scholar. By clicking Rom. 16:1, 3-7, they would receive a description of six or seven women leaders commended by Paul.

Provide mutuality curricula. Much of the responsibility for acknowledging, affirming, and actualizing the calls of women ministers falls on Nazarene senior pastors. Their interpretation of Scripture and attitudes toward women as pastoral colleagues often shape the consensus of congregations. Hence they need the vision of mutuality repeated by Nazarene leadership, pertinent preaching, and teaching tools.

The curricula should reexamine the texts often used to limit women's roles in the church. In light of Paul's overall positive attitude toward women in ministry (note his commendations of women in Acts 18:24-26; Rom. 16:1, 6, 12), his command for silence in 1 Cor. 14 appears to be in response to a specific problem in Corinth. The issue probably was noisy disruption of worship by women. Those who had been denied access to the Scriptures were abusing their newfound freedom to receive and speak truth.

In 1 Tim. 2:11-15, Paul states an injunction against women speaking in church. He adds, "I do not permit a woman to teach or to have authority over a man" (NIV). The rationale given for this prohibition is the "order of creation" of rabbinical tradition. Man has preeminence over the woman because he was created first. This traditionalist view, however, is countered by Paul in 1 Cor. 11:11-12 when he states, "In the Lord woman is not independent of man or man independent of woman. For just as woman came from man, so man comes through woman" (NRSV). In other words, after the first Adam, every man would originate from a woman. "In the Lord," one is not above the other.

Paul seems to offer a second reason to bar women from leadership in 1 Tim. 2:14. Since "the woman being quite deceived, fell into transgression" (NASB), she cannot be trusted with teaching. In Rom. 5:12-14, however, Paul contends that Adam, and not Eve, is responsible for the entrance of sin into the world. Paul neither mentions nor blames Eve for sin.

THE OUTPOURING OF THE HOLY SPIRIT ISSUED A NEW AGE OF MINISTERIAL EQUALITY.

Again, the passages used to limit a woman's ministerial role in the church must be seen in light of both Jesus' and Paul's teaching elsewhere. It is imperative that we carefully study the conditions that prompted the author to issue these directives.

Pastors also need access to texts that support gender mutuality. On the Day of Pentecost, Peter preached from Joel's prophecy that says, "YOUR SONS AND YOUR DAUGHTERS SHALL PROPHESY . . . UPON MY BONDSLAVES, BOTH MEN AND WOMEN, I WILL IN THOSE DAYS POUR FORTH OF MY SPIRIT, and they shall prophesy [proclaim, preach]" (Acts 2:17-18, NASB). These verses indicate the outpouring of the Holy Spirit issued a new age of ministerial equality.

Paul seems to confirm this in his first letter to the Corinthians, by making no distinction between men and women regarding the exercise of spiritual gifts. He writes, "to each is given the manifestation of the Spirit for the common good" (1 Cor. 12:7, NRSV). Limiting a woman's range of expression only divides and impairs the Church. Instead, men and women should rejoice with Paul that in Christ "there is no longer Jew or Greek, there is no longer slave or free, there is no longer male and female; for all of you are one in Christ Jesus" (Gal. 3:28, NRSV).

Acknowledge our Wesleyan tradition, which promotes women in ministry. John Wesley originally opposed allowing women to preach. However, through the influence of his gifted mother, Susanna, the rising need for more lay preachers, and God's apparent anointing on several women speakers, he began to change his mind. He described Mary Fletcher's preaching as "fire, conveying both light and heat to all that heard her."[13]

Adam Clarke, biblical scholar and close Wesley associate, concurred with the promotion of women in ministry, "Under the blessed spirit of Christianity, they have equal rights, equal privileges and equal blessing, and let me add, they are equally useful."[14]

More than 100 years later, J. B. Chapman, general superintendent in the Church of the Nazarene, defended the young denomination's positive stance on women preachers, "The fact is that God calls men and women to preach the gospel, and when He does so call them, they should gladly obey Him and members of the church and of the ministry should encourage and help them in the fulfillment of their task."[15]

> WOMEN WHO ARE CALLED TO PREACH AND LEAD MUST REMAIN FAITHFUL TO THE CALLER.

With or without this encouragement, many early Nazarene women stepped out of their traditional roles in the home to obey God's call to preach. Their ministries, along with the contributions of countless women in a variety of denominations, are an inspiration to women today, who must not hinge their obedience on the church's formal sanction. Women who are called to preach and lead must remain faithful to the Caller.

Our obedience must also be coupled with Christlike love for our opponents. Rather than nursing bitterness over sexual discrimination, we must prayerfully ask God for grace to forgive and to make the most of present opportunities to serve the Kingdom. We must also take advantage of current avenues of support. Newsletters and conferences such as the Come to the Water gathering of more than 500 clergywomen in Wesleyan/Holiness churches provide a rich pool of ministry resources and mutual affirmation.

Every time I approach a Nazarene pulpit, I thank God for the privilege to use my preaching gifts. I am linked to a Judeo-Christian heritage of valiant women who braved condemnation and intense suffering to actively participate in God's redemptive story. Their epitaphs, writings, portraits, and photographs are forever etched in my memory and somehow woven into the way I preach, teach, and pastor. I am also linked to today's women ministers whose faith and servanthood often transcend current streams of sexism.

I am painfully aware of sisters in other denominations who have been denied ordination on the basis that they do not bear a "natural resemblance to Christ," or that they are perennially cursed with Eve's weak temperament and fate of subordination. I empathize now more than ever with their quest for reformation and reconciliation in the Body of Christ.

Their struggle has become mine; even more so since I have chosen to step aside from teaching to become a senior pastor in the Church of the Nazarene. My husband and I want to model the ministerial partnership that characterized so many early Nazarene ministry couples.

From the day my congregation ran to me bestowing the beloved title "Pastor," I have earnestly tried to discern the priorities and perimeters of this divine assignment. I seek:

- the holy boldness of evangelist Estelle Crutcher to preach with power
- the fortitude of missionary Louise Chapman to overcome insurmountable obstacles
- the winsome attitude of missionary Mary Anderson to counter discouragement
- the confidence of pastor Agnes Diffee to expand the vision of my congregation and
- the love of church planter Mary Lee Cagle to gracefully respond to criticism

Remember the author of those letters to undermine my pastoral vote? He now attends worship every Sunday and has become a faithful supporter. I am wise enough to know that I did not change his mind. It was the One who transformed my heart and set my life on a course of glorious love. I am pastor. May many more anointed Nazarene women join me in this holy enterprise.

---

1. *Minutes of the Los Angeles First Church of the Nazarene Incorporation Meeting,* Richard Willis Collection, Point Loma Nazarene University Archives, 30 Oct. 1895, 3.

2. Rebecca Laird, *Ordained Women in the Church of the Nazarene* (Kansas City: Nazarene Publishing House, 1993), 63.

3. Ibid., 46.

4. Ibid., 44.

5. R. Stanley Ingersol, "Knowledge and Vital Piety: Lucia de Costa's Enduring Witness," *Herald of Holiness* (April 1996), 13.

6. Timothy L. Smith, *Called unto Holiness: The Story of the Nazarenes: The Formative Years,* 2nd ed. (Kansas City: Nazarene Publishing House, 1962), 137-38.

7. C. S. Cowles, "In Praise of Women Preachers," Lecture at Northwest Nazarene College, Nampa, Idaho (9 May 1991), 2.

8. Tertullian, "On the Veiling of Virgins," *Ante Nicene Fathers, Vol. 4,* eds. Alexander Roberts and James Donaldson (Peabody, Mass.: Hendrickson Publishers, 1995), 9.

9. C. S. Cowles, *A Woman's Place? Leadership in the Church* (Kansas City: Beacon Hill Press of Kansas City, 1993), 5.

10. Henri J. M. Nouwen, *Creative Ministry* (Garden City, N.Y.: Doubleday, 1978), 81.

11. Gretchen Gaebelein Hull, *Equal to Serve: Women and Men Working Together Revealing the Gospel* (Grand Rapids: Baker, 1991), 218.

12. *Manual: Church of the Nazarene* (Kansas City: Nazarene Publishing House, 2001), par. 904.6.

13. John Wesley, *The Journals of Rev. John Wesley, Vol. 7,* ed. Nehemiah Curnock (London: Epworth, 1938), 247.

14. Quoted in B. T. Roberts, *Ordaining Women* (Rochester, N.Y.: Earnest Christian, 1981), 59.

15. James Blaine Chapman, "October Gleanings," *Herald of Holiness* (15 Oct. 1930), 5.

The clergy are

those particular people

within the whole Church

who have been specially

trained and set aside

to look after

what concerns us as

creatures who are going

to live for ever.

—C. S. Lewis

From *The Quotable Lewis*, eds. Wayne Martindale and Jerry Root (Wheaton: Tyndale House Publishers, Inc., 1989), 112.

4

IF YOU ARE CALLED, NEVER STOOP TO BE A KING

G. B. Williamson

THE VOCATION of the Christian ministry is in a class by itself. It is both a calling and a profession.

It is first of all God's choice. Jesus said, "Ye have not chosen me, but I have chosen you, and ordained you" (John 15:16). To Saul of Tarsus on the Damascus Road, He said, "I have appeared unto thee for this purpose, to make thee a minister and a witness" (Acts 26:16). After Damascus, the apostle Paul always looked upon his work as an assignment from God. To the Galatians, he said, "When it pleased God, who separated me from my mother's womb, and called me by his grace, to reveal his Son in me, that I might preach him among the heathen; immediately I conferred not with flesh and blood" (1:15-16). To the Corinthians, he explained, "I am compelled to preach. Woe to me if I do not preach the gospel! If I preach voluntarily, I have a reward; if not voluntarily, I am simply discharging the trust committed to me" (1 Cor. 9:16-17, NIV).

THE DIVINE CALL:
FOUNDATION FOR EVERY PHASE OF MINISTRY

There are some who have rejected the idea that a divine call is a necessary consideration for entering the ministry. But it is still the only adequate foundation for the largest measure of success in this sacred vocation. Not everyone who is called is forced to choose between preaching the gospel and accepting eternal hell as his everlasting portion. But only he who has the persuasion deep in his soul that preaching is God's first choice for his life will possess the necessary qualifications for a ministry that fulfills God's ideal.

Mission: The awareness of a divine appointment gives one a sense of mission. It urges him on with a divine compulsion. Paul said, "The love of Christ constraineth us." Very naturally the one who looks upon the ministry as a vocation of his own choosing will feel that, since he started by his own appointment, he may quit when he gets ready. That may explain why there are so many ex-preachers now engaged in secular pursuits. To every preacher there come times

WITHOUT THE ASSURANCE OF A DIVINE SANCTION, PREACHERS ARE DISPOSED TO SPEAK APOLOGETICALLY OF THE GOSPEL.

of discouragement when adverse circumstances multiply; but if he can rest back upon the full persuasion that it was in answer to God's call that he took upon himself the work of the ministry, new endurance, faith, and courage will be born in his soul.

Authority: Without the assurance of a divine sanction, preachers are disposed to speak apologetically of the gospel. They indulge in speculation. They cater to the demands of carnal and worldly church members. They soft-pedal the rugged notes of the gospel message that make demands upon the conscience. They dilute the doctrines that are pure and changeless. They think in terms of personal advantage and seek the praise of men. They do not speak with authority. The note of conviction and finality is absent in their pulpit utterances.

Partnership: While a divine mandate is necessary to a large success in this holy calling, yet all the responsibility for fruitful service does not rest upon God. The ministry is a calling. As such, the choice is God's; but it is also a profession and, as such, requires that all who enter its ranks shall give their best to it. Every minister must stir up the gift that is within.

THE PERSONAL RESPONSIBILITY: REQUIRES PREPARATION AND ACCOUNTABILITY

That God has called him is not a substitute for an adequate period of preparation and diligence in maintaining a life disciplined by study and hard work. Paul said to Timothy, "Study to shew thyself approved unto God, a workman that needeth not to be ashamed, rightly dividing the word of truth" (2 Tim. 2:15). Every preacher should place all his capabilities at God's disposal and do his best to be a workman without cause for shame.

Winning Souls: The preacher is not only the custodian of the unsearchable riches of Christ but also charged with the responsibility of saving the souls of men. Jesus placed the value of a soul above that of the whole world. If a preacher trifles with his calling, if he squanders his time, if he defaults his duty, priceless souls will be required at his hands.

Accountability: This great responsibility carries with it the idea of accountability. Preachers are admonished to watch for souls as they that must give account, that they may do it with joy and not with grief. Paul said to Timothy, "I charge thee therefore before God, and the Lord Jesus Christ, who shall judge the quick and the dead at his appearing and his kingdom; preach the word; be instant in season, out of season; reprove, rebuke, exhort with all longsuffering and doctrine . . . do the work of an evangelist, make full proof of thy ministry" (2 Tim. 4:1-2, 5). Preachers tremble at the thought of an annual report. How will they feel when they stand before the great Shepherd and Bishop of their souls to make a final report. Only as one lives with a sense of great responsibility can he anticipate the judgment without fear.

All the scriptural designations for the minister of the gospel imply solemn responsibility to God and man—prophet, priest, servant of God, minister of Christ, man of God, husbandman, bishop, elder, ambassador, angel of the church, shepherd, and overseer of the flock of God. What a vocation, what an assignment, what an obligation belong to all who enter this holy calling!

Certainly none should presume to consider himself worthy of such high honor or equal to such responsibility.

THE UNIQUENESS OF THE PASTORATE AMONG THE MINISTRIES OF THE CHURCH

There are several phases of the ministry, offering place to many persons of various types of mind and personality. Paul recognized this fact. In writing to the Ephesians he said,

> But unto every one of us is given grace according to the measure of the gift of Christ. . . . He gave some, apostles; and some, prophets; and some, evangelists; and some, pastors and teachers; for the perfecting of the saints, for the work of the ministry, for the edifying of the body of Christ: till we all come in the unity of the faith, and of the knowledge of the Son of God, unto a perfect man, unto the measure of the stature of the fulness of Christ . . . From whom the whole body fitly joined together and compacted by that which every joint supplieth, according to the effectual working in the measure of every part, maketh increase of the body unto the edifying of itself in love *(4:7, 11-13, 16).*

In the Church of our day there are evangelists, pastors, teachers, and administrators. They all supplement and support one another. Each one supplies something that is needed to make complete the Body of Christ. None should feel inferior in his appointed place. None should feel superior because some distinctive gift is his. All are joined together in Christ to minister salvation to needy men and build God's kingdom on the earth.

Of the several positions in the Church, the pastorate involves more of the functions of the Christian ministry than any other. In a very real sense a pastor is a preacher, an evangelist, a teacher, and an administrator. To him is given the opportunity to improve his mind and talents by regular habits of study and prayer. He may plan his work and work his plan. He has contact with people and preaches to their need with accurate aim. His task is like that of his Lord and Master. He may say as did Jesus, "The Spirit of the Lord is upon me, because he hath anointed me to preach the gospel to the poor; he hath sent me to heal the brokenhearted, to preach deliverance to the captives, and recovering of sight to the blind, to set at liberty them that are bruised" (Luke 4:18).

He may be engaged in a soul-saving ministry. He may feed the flock of God and witness their growth in the grace and knowledge of the Savior.

No one called of God to the ministry can do better than to begin as pastor of a church. It is the place most suited to an apprenticeship. There the preacher will learn most. His understanding of people will be broadened. His mind and character will gain strength and stability. If he is ever to serve in any specialized field, he needs the firm foundation that pastoring a church will build.

It is difficult to understand why a person who has the soul of a true minister of Christ should ever, by his own volition, leave the pastorate. His restless eagerness to do so may prove he is unfit for the place he fills, but it may also reveal that he is not prepared to fill the place he desires. To urge a young preacher to remain in the pastoral ministry, until an election by the church to some other office is confirmed by unmistakable providences, is sound advice.

GOD SELDOM ALLOWS A PASTOR TO OUTGROW HIS ASSIGNMENT.

If one feels the need of a larger place in which to fulfill his call, there is unlimited opportunity for him to broaden his sphere of influence in his own church and community. God seldom allows a pastor to outgrow his assignment. As the pastor grows, the opportunity enlarges. Much more frequent is the predicament of a small preacher trying to do a job too big to handle. If he is aware of the ill-proportioned situation, he will be embarrassed. If unaware of it, he will be held in contempt by others.

To be sure, a full consecration to do the whole will of God is necessary. One must recognize the call of duty when that inner voice speaks and, at whatever sacrifice, he must respond by saying, "The will of the Lord be done." But a person who has a call to preach can more nearly find all his heart longs for in pastoring a church than anywhere else. He should assume that a call to the ministry will lead him into the place in which he can develop his own mind and soul according to the pattern set before him in Christ Jesus, in which he can in the most natural way serve God and his fellowmen, and in which he can do the most for the building of God's kingdom. The rule is that such a place is the pastorate. Any exceptions prove the rule rather than disprove it.

After all, who knows how far-reaching a pastor's influence may be? He may make the work both intensive and extensive. He may give attention to the spirituality of his church. He may evangelize a community. Directly or indirectly he may make his influence reach other nearby communities and ultimately the ends of the earth. The offerings that his people make unto God may help send the gospel into all the world. The lives consecrated to the service of God under his ministry may become God's chosen vessels to bear His name to the most distant places.

It is to such humble, faithful, God-called servants of the Church that this chapter is directed.

THE PERSON

Next to the grace of God, a pastor's personality is the greatest factor in his success. That statement is not based upon any superficial measurement of the pastor. The fact that he is a good showman or even a good salesman does not define his personality. It is not only the impression made upon the first meeting but also how well he wears in a long acquaintance. It recognizes not only the reputation gained in the estimation of men but also the character he possesses in the sight of the all-seeing God.

Personality includes the whole person, physical, intellectual, moral, and spiritual. What one attains in personal charm, intelligence, strength, and god-like capacity will determine one's accomplishment in the service of God and the church. His work will be the true measure of the pastor. His influence as a spiritual leader can never be any greater than his own attainments would indicate.

In this discussion of the pastor's personality, let us begin with those things that are most peripheral and proceed to things central. But let none suppose that even the things that have to do with outward appearance are unimportant. They not only have bearing upon impressions received by others; they also reveal what there is buried in the deeper strata of a pastor's life.

THE MINISTER'S APPEARANCE

First, then, let it be said, without apology, that the personal appearance of a pastor is important. A few ministers who have been careless about their personal appearance have succeeded to some degree, but their scarcity should be a warning to all who are tempted deliberately to follow their example. Possibly extraordinary powers of mind carried such pastors to success. None should presume to be possessed of such capabilities.

> THE PERSONAL APPEARANCE OF A PASTOR IS IMPORTANT.

Therefore, a pastor should give attention to the manner of his dress. He need not wear a distinctive clerical garb. He should not feel himself above putting on work clothes if the occasion demands, and he need not fear to soil his hands with manual labor. But when he presents himself for public appearance on the street, in society, or in the church service, he should be as presentable as the profession of the ministry requires.

A preacher's clothing need not be costly. It cannot always be new. It should never be extravagant or out of harmony with the circumstances in which he finds himself. He should not look as if he had just emerged from the tailor's shop, while his spouse and family are shabby. He should not dress in such a way as to make parishioners self-conscious; but under all circumstances a pastor should be clean, neat, and well-groomed. Even well-worn clothes can be spotless and pressed. Soap, water, cleaning fluid, a clothes brush, shoe polish, and a pressing iron can all be had for very little and they can do wonders in keeping a preacher respectable in appearance.

But the clothes do not make the preacher. The rack on which they hang is significant too. Hair should be neatly combed, face and hands washed, and fingernails free of dirt. He should cultivate a becoming posture, with shoulders erect. Whether sitting or standing, he should avoid careless and vulgar positions. He should combat excessive weight by disciplined habits of eating and by physical exercise. He should take all proper precautions against body odors and offensive breath. His teeth should receive necessary care, in order to preserve them, as well as for best appearance.

THE MINISTER'S HEALTH

The pastor's body is the temple of God's Spirit and an instrument consecrated to God for His service. Therefore, all reasonable efforts should be made to keep it well. Indulgence in eating and at irregular hours has undermined the health of many preachers and brought them to an untimely end. Eating three times a day at regular hours and with moderation is a safeguard to good health. Heavy eating late at night is all but suicidal.

Sleep is also necessary to health and a pastor's best performance. Eleven o'clock is a reasonable hour for retirement. Then he will be ready to rise no later than seven in the morning, refreshed in body and mind for another day's work for his Lord and Savior.

There are many things concerning the pastor's health that cannot be discussed here. Suffice it to say that all the well-known rules for personal hygiene should be observed. These should be supplemented by an occasional visit to a reputable doctor for a complete checkup and a semiannual visit to a dentist.

THE MINISTER'S CONDUCT

The third consideration in the measure of a preacher's personality is manners. He does not need to be bound by all the conventions of elite society to the extent that he is unnatural and ill at ease. Nevertheless, it is inexcusable for a pastor to be crude and boorish. He should cultivate the ability to be at ease in polite society. This does not mean that he will feel superior to others. To call attention to their lack of culture would be an evidence of a deficiency in refinement on his own part. A mark of gentility is the ability to put everyone at ease regardless of social standing. An air of superiority and obliging condescension is unnecessary and unbecoming. A natural, unassumed grace and easy bearing are the best evidence of good breeding.

It is especially desirable for a pastor to be able to sit down to anybody's table and eat without embarrassing himself or the host and hostess. Some familiarity with table etiquette is therefore necessary. One may not care to memorize all the rules that Emily Post has laid down, but to be informed on the best procedures at mealtime may save some humiliating experiences. To be sure, if he lives carelessly below his own knowledge at home, he will not be relaxed and comfortable when a guest in another's home. For his own sake and for the sake of his family, appropriate table decorum should be maintained at all meals and every day.

> COURTESY AND DEFERENCE TO ALL PEOPLE ARE APPROPRIATE FOR A PASTOR.

It is also very important that a pastor shall know how to meet strangers and how to introduce them to others. He may not cater to the people who are socially superior, but he should be able to meet anyone without constraint. He should be able to call in the poorest or the best homes in his community with becoming ease.

Courtesy and deference to all people are appropriate for a pastor. Gracious manners will be a very good recommendation for any representative of Christ. Paul said, "Be courteous"; and the psalmist said, "Thy gentleness hath made me great."

Among the graces that a pastor should cultivate is that of gratitude. He is the recipient of many favors. He should never allow himself to take it for granted that they are due him. If it be a kindly word of encouragement or a gift of real worth, it should be acknowledged promptly and appropriately. The pastor should never allow himself to expect gratuities or notice the fact that they are not forthcoming; but when they are received he should let his thanks be expressed in unmistakable ways, whether the consideration be great or small.

A pastor should seek to be a good conversationalist. To be prepared for such a role he should read with some breadth of interest. He should be in command of a good vocabulary and know how to use the language he speaks with intelligence and accuracy. He should avoid egocentric conversation. His clothes, furniture, car, position, travels, attainments, education, family tree, and ailments can become very threadbare topics for discussion. He should be a good listener as well as a good talker. A one-sided visit soon becomes boring. Let the conversation be of things of mutual interest.

The indulgence in gossip about other people should always be beneath the pastor's level. Mean people talk about others, to their own discredit. A pastor should never be a talebearer and he should never leave anyone thinking less of another. If he does, it may be himself.

Little people talk about things. Such conversation may easily become meaningless chatter with a multitude of words, in which sin is not lacking. Big people talk about ideas and ideals. Their speech is with grace, seasoned with salt. Their conversation is in heaven or could be without being out of place. They elevate themselves in the minds of others, and those with whom they speak are elevated too. Here again the use of this kind of conversation in the pastor's own home and with the members of his family will make it more natural elsewhere. And for the sake of his own family, it should be practiced. Many preachers' children have become confirmed critics of others, if not unbelieving rebels, because they have heard so much gossip at home.

THE MINISTER'S SPIRIT

But the most important factor in an engaging personality is one's spirit. There are some pastors who are by innate tendency of even temperament and agreeable disposition. They have an advantage if all else be equal. But there is no reason for one who is not so fortunate to exercise his bad spirit by admitting that he has an unattractive disposition by nature and assuming there is nothing he can do about it. The grace of God will do wonders for him if appropriated by faith.

SELF-DISCIPLINE IN COOPERATION WITH GRACE WILL MAKE A NEW PERSON OF THE MINISTER.

Furthermore, self-discipline in cooperation with grace will make a new person of the minister. One need not yield to the caprice of his own temperament. A suspicious person can cultivate confidence in others. One disposed to melancholy can become cheerful. A pessimistic soul can voluntarily look on the bright side. An introvert can become friendly and an extrovert can, by his own will, become deep-souled and spiritually-minded. Let no person consent to be a victim of his own excesses. With the ideal life of Jesus Christ before him and by the power of God's Spirit working in him, he may become a well-poised and attractive personality.

THE MINISTER'S UNDERSTANDING OF THE TASK

Every preacher should work out for himself a fundamental philosophy of life that is soundly Christian. If one does not think through to such a working philosophy for the guidance of his own spirit, his decisions and judgments will be warped and his attitudes wrong. He will soon be ill-adjusted within himself and out of joint with people in general.

Humility, or a modest estimate of one's own worth, is at bottom in a Christian philosophy of life. If one can truly feel that everything good that he possesses is a gift from God and that a place of trust among people is more than he deserves, it will contribute largely to peace of mind and effectiveness in service. Jesus said, "Whosoever of you will be chiefest, shall be servant of all." And of himself, He said, "I am among you as he that serveth." Paul said, "Unto me, who am less than the least of all saints, is this grace given, that I should preach among the Gentiles the unsearchable riches of Christ." He also said, "Let this mind be in you, which was also in Christ Jesus." Every pastor should consider himself the servant of the Church for Christ's sake. He is appropriately called the minister.

Humility is not voluntarily assumed. It is unconsciously possessed. It is a hidden light that illumines all the virtues of a radiant personality. It not only saves one from egotism with the obvious strut and swagger; it also delivers one from the tendency to be egoistic, and to relate every problem that arises to his own promotion or demotion. It gives him a holy carelessness about what happens to him personally. It enables him to live for the sake of others and for the glory of God. John the Baptist said of Christ, "He must increase, but I must decrease." But Jesus said of John, "He was a burning and a shining light." A preacher of humble mind can trust God for all the future years. God will see to it that he is not overlooked, underrated, or unrewarded.

Charity is a grace complementary to humility. As certainly as one looks upon himself without pride and conceit, he will look upon others with charity for their shortcomings and with appreciation for their good qualities; whereas one who appraises himself too highly will be disposed to discount others in order that he may maintain his own relative position.

This charity-humility combination will go far toward establishing one as a spiritual leader in the confidence of others. A certain self-reliance is needed for spiritual leadership, but Samuel Chadwick gives three rules for one to follow in maintaining such a relation to others. They are: first, self-abnegation; second, self-abnegation; third, self-abnegation. Then the complement to that state of mind is appreciation of others. A faultfinding, critical pastor is doomed to failure. The ability to see his own faults and admit them and the willingness to correct his mistakes and misjudgments are important beyond possibility of overestimation. At the same time, the ability to overlook faults and mistakes of others and to appreciate them is equally important.

A Christian philosophy enables one to live a life of contentment wherever he may be placed. He has forever resigned himself to the will of God. And he knows that "all things work together for good to them that love God, to them who are the called according to his purpose." Resignation to God's will is the secret of contentment. No person who is complaining of his lot, blaming others for his failures, and even feeling that God has not dealt squarely with him, can succeed in the ministry. Ill-content disqualifies one to do anything to change the situation. Submission to God's good and holy will makes him ready to do miracles to bring to pass a happier state of affairs for himself and prepares him for greater service in days to come.

Contentment is not a passive acceptance of the status quo. Dr. Merton S. Rice preached a sermon on "The Discontented Optimist." Such a person knows things could be worse and is glad they are not. He also knows they can be better, and he is prepared to improve them with God's help.

Thus one develops a positive state of mind. Nothing can more certainly predict one's failure than for him to allow himself to be habitually negative in his outlook. Such a one is already a defeated victim of circumstances. Faith in God and His providences, faith in one's fellowmen, and a permissible measure of faith in oneself is the cure for the negative attitude. The positive state of mind makes everything possible.

This Christian philosophy gives one enthusiasm for life, for people with whom one works, and for the task assigned. A passive, phlegmatic soul who has no zest for living and no zeal to serve God and humanity should never enter the ministry. If he finds himself there, he had better change his state of mind or his vocation. Every preacher in a big place or a little one must keep the romance in his work or he can never master the situations by which he will be confronted. Enthusiasm may sometimes lead him beyond the bounds of well-balanced reason, but he will usually be forgiven for being too enthusiastic. The passive soul will never need forgiveness except for living, for he will never do anything. The only way to make sure of never making any blunders is to do nothing.

The pastor who works according to the Christian philosophy may fail sometimes, but not for long. His spirit will enable him to turn failure into success and defeat into victory. It will help him change his opposition into faithful support. It will keep him happy in making others happy.

Adapted from the preface and first chapter of *Overseers of the Flock: A Discussion of Pastoral Practice* (Kansas City: Beacon Hill Press, 1952), 13-28.

People make

themselves available

to pastors

who

have made

themselves available

to

the people.

—William H. Willimon

From *Concise Encyclopedia of Preaching,* eds. William H. Willimon and Richard Lischer (Louisville, Ky.: Westminster John Knox Press, 1995), 363.

5

MINISTRY MEANS SERVING PEOPLE

R. T. Williams

THE PASTOR IS THE HUMAN LEADER, the guide, and the shepherd of the people. The pastor is supposed to be a definitely called and commissioned person, trained for leadership and soul saving. Possibly no one lives of whom more is required and who carries more responsibility.

THE PASTOR'S MINISTRY AMONG PEOPLE

First, he is a preacher. He is called and trained to preach and must be able to do so effectively to succeed in the ministry. The pulpit is the minister's setting for ministry. Whatever he does or does not do, he is a preacher. He is that first, last, and all the time.

I once recommended a very capable man to a congregation for pastor. I was dealing specifically with the church board. I told the board at length of this man's qualifications, especially emphasizing his educational achievements. I told them that he had completed high school, that he had gone through college, obtaining the bachelor of arts degree, that he had gone to the university and there had obtained his master's degree, that he had gone to a famous theological seminary and obtained a degree there, that he had done considerable work on his doctor of philosophy degree, and that in addition to all of this, he was a splendid teacher and Spirit-filled. After telling these board members that this particular man had almost enough diplomas to paper a room, one brother slowly asked, "Can he preach?" This man was right. That question should be asked concerning every preacher. "Can he preach?" If he cannot preach, he is not a preacher. He is something else.

Soon his pews will be empty, and those who stand by do so from a sense of loyalty, which is right, not because they enjoy the sermons. Visitation, courtesy, and love for the people are essential concomitants, but neither these nor other things can ever take the place of the pulpit and sermon. God speaks to the people through the voice of the preacher. After the labor and toil of the week, they come to the house of God for a message from heaven. They must not be disappointed. To meet this responsibility, the pastor should pray and study in preparation to stand before the people.

Second, a preacher must be a specialist in religion. It is not only required of him that he influence others to be religious, he must himself be a living example of the entire gospel he preaches. It is one thing to preach, another to practice. The statement "Do not as I do, but do as I say" will not stand the test of the ministry. The preacher must not only preach high spiritual standards but also possess them in his own character and life, that others may see the embodiment of the virtues he advocates.

> THE PREACHER HAS TO CREATE AN ATMOSPHERE IN THE CHURCH AND AMONG HIS PEOPLE THAT MAKES IT EASY FOR THEM TO GIVE.

Third, the preacher is a financier. The idea, entirely too common, that the preacher has no business ability is unjust and indefensible. The preacher is a businessman; otherwise he cannot finance his church. Regardless of the ability of a church board or the efficiency of a board of stewards, the preacher has to create an atmosphere in the church and among his people that makes it easy for them to give their money for the support of the church. Rightly understood, this is the highest type of salesmanship known. It does not require great ability to sell an automobile when the car is needed and wanted. The preacher has to talk the people into a frame of mind and heart where they will give their money, receiving nothing in return more than consolation and ease of conscience for having done their duty.

The facts are that the preachers of our church and all other churches have made a far better showing in financial leadership than many bankers of the country. During the dark depression days only a few hundred churches became bankrupt, while banks failed by the thousands. I defend the preacher against the slander that he is a poor businessman. He cannot be slothful in business and succeed in the ministry.

To raise money is no easy task. It requires not only ability but also courage. Sad to say, the last thing that people put on the altar is their money, and it is usually the first thing taken off. If a congregation is sensitive, it will be so at this point. It is easy to offend people in pressing them to do their duty in matters financial, but the preacher is obliged to do his duty. This requires skill and a fearless heart. Being human, he craves the goodwill of everybody and recoils from all thought of wounding his friends. Still he must do his duty. The very layperson who finds fault with him for pressing church finances would be the first to criticize if the church could not meet its obligations. A pastor must finance his church, which can be done only through the generosity of his God-fearing people.

Fourth, the preacher is a soul winner. If he is not, he is in the wrong job. He is a worker sent into the harvest field with the ripened grain, to cut the products of the field. If he saves no grain, he is not worthy of his hire. The preacher is a soul winner. If he saves no souls, he is only a club leader—or a manipulator of a sociological group. He dare not fail to lead people to Jesus Christ in definite salvation.

Humanity is sick physically, mentally, and spiritually. Few people are absolutely well. Some need a doctor for sick bodies. Others need a psychiatrist for mental complexes and reactions, while still others need the touch of God for soul ills. I sometimes wish I were a physician, a psychiatrist, and a preacher all in one. Why? To be better able to diagnose all diseases. The doctor is inclined to blame all troubles on a sick body. The psychiatrist traces all troubles to a disordered mind. The preacher traces human ills to a wrong will or a carnal heart. All are partly right and somewhat wrong. The body often needs help, the mind is frequently off center, and many souls need a divine cleansing.

> HUMANITY IS SICK PHYSICALLY, MENTALLY, AND SPIRITUALLY.

The altar is an important place, but it is not the cure for all human ills. Salvation comes nearer to being the remedy for all human disease, physical, mental, and spiritual, than any other. It helps the body. It corrects many mental complexes. It cures the soul of sin. Nevertheless it is a mistake to think a trip to the altar makes every man whole in the full sense of that concept. Not long ago I dealt with a young woman who had been to the altar repeatedly and was discouraged. Her trouble was mental. I helped her to see that wrong conceptions of truth were the unsettling influences in her soul. Seeing this, she was immediately able to exercise that faith essential to a triumphant experience and life.

If the preacher could only see that he is often dealing with sick people instead of mean, or stubborn people, he would be far more patient and efficient in his work. Charity would take the place of hard, legalistic attitudes so quick to condemn. One's trouble might be traceable to a sinful soul or to a sick mind or to shattered nerves. To properly diagnose each patient is an art to be coveted.

Fifth, a pastor is an adviser and counselor. People come to him for about everything except the removal of the appendix or a brain operation. In fact if he is not a surgeon, he is a psychiatrist. If he does not deal with the brain, at least he deals with the mind. The most intimate things of life are revealed to the preacher and to the doctor. If there is any difference, the preacher is led into more of the secrets of the people than the doctor. The counsel given by the preacher, in the main, must be sound. He cannot always be correct, but his average must be good. In other words, he must succeed more often than he fails in helping people solve their most delicate, intimate, and perplexing problems.

It is a high compliment to a pastor for his people or the public to feel safe in revealing to him their spiritual needs. This is evidence of confidence in his integrity and judgment. They believe that he can help them and that he will keep their secrets as a sacred trust. Many a preacher has done himself and others great harm by being unethical at this point. Secrets are revealed to him that should never be divulged even to his own family. For a preacher to be unethical in this sacred matter disqualifies him for the highest type of spiritual leadership.

Sixth, the preacher is a mixer and a leader. The ministry is no place for a hermit or an introvert. I do not mean, by this, that he should have none of the characteristics of the mystic or introvert, but I mean that he must have enough of the extrovert to make him balanced, so that he can live not only within the cloister of his own mind, but equally as well without. In his study he can be a student and there enter into the holy of holies with God. When he comes from his study he must mix with the multitude, weeping with those who weep and rejoicing with those who rejoice, knowing how to make contact with the public.

An unfriendly person will not win friends. If any substitution could be made successfully for preaching, it would be friendliness. The former is the chief means of mass evangelism, the latter an essential to personal evangelism. Sinners usually admire the personality of the preacher before he can lead them to Christ.

It would be impossible to use the space here to enumerate all of the requirements and qualifications of the preacher that are essential to success in his holy calling. Therefore we have mentioned only a few.

Possibly nothing is more important in the preacher than the ability to keep the right relationship between himself and the people whom he serves. How can this be done?

THE ATTITUDE OF THE PREACHER TOWARD THE PEOPLE

A proper relationship between pastor and people is made possible only by a right attitude of one toward the other.

It is obvious that no one but the pastor can determine what his attitude will be. This is his own exclusive and personal responsibility. Jesus emphasized in one terse statement the full responsibility of the pastor to his people, "A good shepherd giveth his life for the sheep."

This statement implies love, love in the heart of the shepherd for his sheep, a love so deep, and high, and broad that it will protect the sheep unto death. A minister to succeed in his leadership of the people must not endure them but love them. I once heard a man say he would rather associate with animals than with people. That was his natural disposition. The grace of God had changed him. Otherwise he would have been utterly impotent in his calling. The sheep know the feeling of the shepherd toward them. If he has hatred in his heart, they will know it. If he is indifferent, they will know it. If he loves them, they will know it. It is impossible for one's attitude toward another to be concealed. It will show itself in the eye or in the gesture or in one's acts. If not in these ways, it will at least be interpreted by one's spirit. We often feel what we cannot see or hear. There is an unexplained communication between personalities. Behind the mask of a hypocritical smile and handshake is felt the coldness of an unfriendly spirit.

People who sit in the congregation before the preacher do three things, at least. First, they look at him, his form and face, his clothes, the color of his hair, and his gestures. They take into consideration his entire appearance. Second, they hear what he says or at least pretend to, and I think they usually do, for when the preacher says something that is questionable the people always seem to catch it. They look at the preacher and they hear him. Third, they feel his personality. I sometimes think what they feel has more effect upon them than what they see and hear.

WHAT A PREACHER IS CAN NEVER BE CONCEALED FROM THE CONGREGATION.

What a preacher is can never be concealed from the congregation. They know him far better possibly than he thinks. The humblest person of a local church, though unacquainted with logic and the principles of psychology, can interpret effectively the spirit of a preacher. Every preacher should bear in mind at all times that people look at him, hear him, and feel him. Reading and listening to the radio are less effective than hearing the preacher deliver his message. The reader can only read. He cannot see the writer nor can he feel him, with any degree of satisfaction. The listener to the radio can hear but cannot feel the speaker. The members of the congregation can hear and see the speaker and effectively feel the impact of his spirit and the power of his personality. If the preacher loves them, they will see it, hear it, and feel it.

One of the most beautiful statements delivered by our Lord is this, "My sheep know my voice." It is evident that this quality, which makes for understanding, is love.

For many years I read the following statement with little effect. "Even as I have loved you so love ye one another." One day I read the statement with understanding and was shocked and convicted, because I felt in my heart that I was not living up to the true meaning and full import of this statement. "Even as I have loved you so love ye one another." I readily concede that the command given here applies to all Christians, whether laypersons or ministers, but it seems to me that it has special significance for the minister of the gospel, the shepherd of the sheep. If Christians generally are obliged to love one another to this extent, it would certainly be mandatory for the preacher to love the people in this measure.

In my judgment a burning passion of love in the heart of the preacher for the members of his congregation is the first essential of success. His love must be deep and broad enough to reach everyone—the faithful and the unfaithful, the loyal and the disloyal, those easily entreated and the stubborn, the lovable and the unlovable, the rich and the poor, the educated and the illiterate; his love must apply to all.

The preacher must not only love his people but be willing and ready to sacrifice for them. With this statement I have no little difficulty, for it is questionable whether sacrifice is possible in the presence of love. In other words, sacrifice made in love ceases to be sacrifice. No father or mother will consider service to a child sacrificial, however great the self-denial might be. Nevertheless, there is unquestionably a sacrificial element in the ministry. The statement stands that "a good shepherd giveth his life for the sheep." He is always ready to step between them and danger. If division arises over him, he will step down and out, being ready and willing to be sacrificed if such sacrifice can save his people. If he is opposed, rightly or wrongly, he would rather suffer than have his people break fellowship on his account. Trouble can be expected sooner or later in any local church where the preacher is not willing to sacrifice himself in the interest of his people. All preachers will admit this readily, but not all will act accordingly in the crisis. The unselfish will, while others will contend that it is to the best interest of the church for them to remain. In case of disagreement or division, the selfish pastor will claim that the people who are not for him are carnal and troublemakers, that they have run other preachers off, and if he leaves they will treat the next one in like manner. And in some cases he is correct, but he should be willing to listen to advice from his district or general superintendent or others not personally concerned in the situation.

THE PREACHER IS THE SERVANT OF THE PEOPLE.

The consecration of every true minister includes the possibility of his own personal humiliation and loss in the interest of those whom he serves. The Good Shepherd loves His sheep and makes that fact known to them by His willingness to lay down His life in their behalf.

The preacher is the servant of the people. Is this not implied in the statement, "A good shepherd giveth his life for the sheep"? Love is included. Sacrifice is included. Service is included. The shepherd watches over the sheep day and night. He leads them into green pastures and beside the still waters. He is their servant.

Yes, the preacher is true shepherd of the sheep. He is always ready to help those who need the assistance he is able to give. The man or the woman unwilling to serve should never disgrace the sacred calling of the ministry.

The true pastor is absorbed in the interests of his people. He has a right to happiness and the comforts of life. At the same time, his consecration to this holy ministry requires him to sacrifice himself, if such becomes necessary for the salvation and happiness of the people. He cannot think too much about himself and succeed. His position must be on the altar, so he will not be thinking of the day of recall. One rule should govern his entire life, the rule of duty. He should fear to do wrong but should never quail when facing duty. If I were to advise a minister, it would be this, "Do your duty at all times and accept the consequences." The weakness of the politician is his fear of displeasing certain voters. This constant fear is a handicap to him in the performance of efficient and conscientious duty. If every office holder in the municipal, state, and national governments would do his duty, thinking only of the good of the people instead of his own welfare, our country always would be safe. This same principle may be applied to the preacher.

The minister who loves God and immortal souls and is dedicated to the performance of duty, never worrying about himself, is likely to have less trouble in his relationships with the people than a person who is concerned for his own protection and promotion. The minister who loves his congregation commensurate with the command of Jesus, that we should love one another as He loved us, will escape many of those personal difficulties common between pastor and people.

A PASTOR MUST BE WORTHY OF THE CONFIDENCE OF THE PEOPLE.

A pastor must be worthy of the confidence of the people. He has no right to demand respect from them unless he is worthy of respect. He has no right to expect them to follow him unless he is worthy of their confidence. Any leader must recognize the two aspects of leadership. Commands should be obeyed. However it is the duty of the commander to give orders that are reasonable, just, and right. The preacher is ordinarily a person of strong convictions and may be misled into thinking that every incidental matter is a fundamental issue in which he must take his stand.

One principle will always serve as a very safe guide when one is in doubt: Eliminate self-interest and think only of those whom one serves. An unselfish heart usually is possessed of wisdom, but a selfish mind is blind, even to its own best interest.

I have heard ministers abuse the people for not coming out to the preaching services or find fault because their ministry did not seem to be acceptable. Why so? Those being served at the table, who do not relish the food set before them, may be in need of a physician; however, the lack of appetite may be due to the poor quality of food or service.

If people do not enjoy the sermons preached by the pastor, they may be at fault or the pastor may be at fault. In such cases the wise preacher will first investigate himself carefully before finding fault with his people.

One of the common complaints made against a Nazarene preacher who is not succeeding is his failure to feed the people. You have heard this expression, "We are starving to death." It has been my observation over years of experience with our people that the average layperson of the Church of the Nazarene is hungry for the true gospel and does not object to straight preaching. He wants the truth, the whole truth, and nothing but the truth. He may object to some pet notion or personal opinion of the preacher, but his mind and heart are open to the Word of God. If he did not want the truth, it is unlikely he would be identified with a church of such high standards.

Every preacher has a right to expect the full cooperation of the membership of his church in all things, financial and spiritual, but in return must himself be worthy of their wholehearted cooperation.

This requires that the character of the preacher embody Christian graces, such as love, kindness, courtesy, humility, longsuffering, mercy, justice, purity, and unselfishness. He has a right to expect the people to follow him when they find within him those Christian characteristics that inspire admiration, confidence, and courage. What he is stands out so prominently that it has a pronounced effect upon everything he says.

> **A PASTOR MIGHT BE MORALLY AND ETHICALLY GOOD AND YET VERY INEFFECTIVE AS A LEADER.**

His life must be exemplary. "Follow me as I follow Christ," is a good rule for the life of any good Christian, especially the preacher. "Be thou an example of the believers in word, in conversation, in charity, in spirit, in faith, in purity." This includes the whole activity of a Christian.

Much is involved in the leadership of the pastor. It is not enough for him to be unimpeachable in character. A pastor might be morally and ethically good and yet very ineffective as a leader. Vision is required in leadership. A pastor might want to do and yet see nothing to do. Have you not heard pastors say something like this: "I have gone about as far with these people I can go. There seems to be nothing else for me to do"? When the pastor feels this way, he should move. Without vision the people perish. Leadership implies vision that is easily misinterpreted. Vision in reality is seeing what ought to be done, what can be done, and a way to do it. Leadership must not fall very far short of this high goal. A leader must keep a step ahead of his followers. He must be able to see something to do and a way to do it. Thus he is able to inspire his people with courage and keep their energies constantly employed. A church, to be progressive, must be given a vision and inspired to intense activity. The hope for this lies in the preacher, who is the leader.

Leadership implies wisdom. A leader is not expected to be infallible. The only pastor who never makes a mistake is he who does nothing. Only the dead are free from errors. It is better to do something imperfectly than to do nothing. The fewer the mistakes made the better, for mistakes in leadership are essentially a handicap to progress. One must be sufficiently wise in leadership to lift him above the line of mediocrity. The importance of wisdom is taught in the Scriptures. We are invited to pray for wisdom. The New Testament exhorts Christians to pray for leaders in civil government, for wisdom is needed in leadership, whether in government or religion.

Leadership implies unselfishness. This we have stated before but repeat for emphasis. "Whosoever will be great among you, let him be your minister." The pastor who can inspire the people by the quality of his character, by the high ethical standards of his life, and by his wise and unselfish leadership is bound to succeed. The leader has a right to expect the cooperation of his congregation, and at the same time the people in the congregation have a right to demand of him those qualities that inspire confidence.

Have we considered the value of laypersons? What could we ministers do without them? They feed and clothe our families, educate our children, furnish us homes and cars to drive. They give us the opportunity to carry out our divine commission. They love us, pray for us, and give us the finest atmosphere and fellowship the world has for ourselves and our families.

There is no group like Christian people, filled with the Spirit and devoted to God and Christian service. Let no pastor speak lightly of our God-fearing laypersons. They are the most wonderful people on earth, loyal, devoted, earnest, sacrificial, and a most pleasant group to lead and serve.

How often would I have been discouraged, and tempted to quit the fight, if I had not seen before me that crowd of loyal souls looking at me as if they believed in me and were counting on my faithfulness. Fail them? No, not for the world. What do we owe them? The best we have, all we have. They believe our message and follow our leadership.

True, there are a few, very few, laypersons, who are not spiritual, troublemakers. This group is so overshadowed by that great majority who would follow Christ and the pastor to death, they really become inconsequential. Why listen to one poor fellow who is never happy, but faultfinding, when there are scores who would give and do give their very all to promote the gospel they love? Is this boasting, when we praise these faithful members of the church? Yes, we are boasting in the Lord, for these are the products of the glorious gospel of our Lord. The glory is to Him now and forever.

Adapted from chapters 3 and 4 of *Pastor and People* (Kansas City: Nazarene Publishing House, 1939), 15-34.

What we need is a revival of

pastoral ministry

as defined by

Almighty God . . .

If we want the church

to make a difference in our

increasingly secular society,

we cannot look

to that society for instruction.

The answers—*real* answers,

practical answers—are

still to be found only

in God's Word.

—E. Glenn Wagner

From *Escape from Church, Inc.* (Grand Rapids: Zondervan Publishing House, 1999), 69.

6

SELF-FORGETFUL, CHRIST-EXALTING LEADERSHIP

Eugene L. Stowe

IF THE CONGREGATION is to enjoy the delights of green pastures and still waters, it must be led there by the pastor-shepherd. This is a sobering responsibility. Like Moses and Gideon, most ministers feel incapable of filling this role. But God's call provides the necessary assurance that He sees potential leadership in those whom He has summoned to the shepherding task. Diligent application to the development of effective skills will produce satisfactory proficiency in this area.

President Dwight D. Eisenhower's book *At Ease* should be required reading for every minister. From a very modest beginning, he rose to the highest level of both military and political leadership. He gives this profile of the basic qualities of the successful leader:

> Men who can do things are going to be sought out just as surely as the sun rises in the morning. Fake reputations, habits of glib and clever speech, and glittering surface performances are going to be discovered and kicked overboard! Solid, sound leadership with inexhaustible nervous energy to spur the efforts of lesser men, and ironclad determination to face discouragement, risk, and increasing work without flinching are imperative. Added to this he must have a strong tinge of imagination. . . . Finally, he must be able to forget himself and his personal fortunes.[1]

How interesting that this description of secular leadership should climax with the necessity of self-forgetfulness. If this is true in the army and in the government, how much truer it is in the church. It is the kiss of death for a preacher's work to betray any indication of self-serving or political motivation. There is a place for legitimate ministerial aspiration, but it must always be genuinely sanctified ambition. After 50 years of evangelistic ministry, Dr. Vance Havner could write: "No man with God's message need politick, nor pull wires, nor sit hunched over cafeteria tables making contacts, nor wait for some talent scout to find him. He need not chase key men around if he knows the Keeper of the Keys!"[2]

This eminent Southern Baptist testifies to the infilling of the Holy Spirit as a second crisis experience and identifies this as the enablement for self-effacing, Christ-exalting service.[3] If the cleansing of the heart means anything, it means a sublime release from carnal concern about personal ministerial fortunes.

AUTHORITY—RIGHT AND WRONG

A careful reading of the New Testament reveals that authority, in itself, is not wrong. We have allowed some unfortunate connotations of authority as exercised in our world to color our thinking on this subject. Authority in the church is different from that outside it, basically because of *the way the leader exercises authority*. This begins with the *servant role*. Jesus spelled this out in Matt. 20:25-27: "Ye know that the princes of the Gentiles exercise dominion over them, and they that are great exercise authority upon them. But it shall not be so among you: but whosoever will be great among you, let him be your minister; and whosoever will be chief among you, let him be your servant." This concept is unique and adds a fundamental dimension to the exercise of leadership in the church. No true shepherd should ever forget it.

Then, the minister's authority is *self-authenticating*. As a God-called leader, his life and ministry will document his authority. His authority rests in his ordination by God and in the faithfulness with which he lives and teaches his message. The authority is intrinsic. Thus the Christian leader has no need to demand or to scheme, to politick or to plot.[4]

Successful leadership is contingent upon the ability to find the median between two equally dangerous aberrations:

1. The autocratic, dictatorial abuse of authority. David Redding reminds us that "Joseph's hardest test was power. The life of slavery, the temptations of women were little things compared to the peril of sinning with the scepter."[5] Evidently the apostle Peter sensed this problem area in the Early Church. In his timeless advices to elders he cautions against "lording it over" your charges (1 Pet. 5:3, NASB). Dag Hammarskjöld was entrusted with one of the most crucial assignments in recent history when he was elected the first secretary-general of the United Nations. His pattern of leadership was exemplary. Out of this experience he wrote, "Position never gives out the right to command. It only imposes the duty of so living that others can receive your orders without being humiliated."[6] The basic difference here is between leading and driving. Tyrants and despots drive. Real leaders lead.

A safeguard against this temptation to autocracy is *seeing the ministerial office not as special privilege but rather as a responsibility of privilege*. It must be properly related to the scriptural chain of command. Christ is the Head of the Church, and all ecclesiastical authority derives from living under His Lordship. Through the ordination commitment the minister places himself under the authority of the church as administered through its duly constituted leadership. In turn the local congregation relates itself to the properly constituted pastoral authority. A lack of respect for and responsibility to the higher level of authority in each case will result in anarchy with its attendant evils. The pastor who disregards the supervision of his denominational superiors creates a climate of disrespect in his church that will ultimately lead to a lack of regard for his leadership on the part of his parishioners.

2. *Failure to assume the proper stance of leadership.* This peril is just as dangerous as the first. It may cloak itself in an honest attempt to display genuine Christian humility. However, if this commendable effort results in a leadership vacuum, dire consequences will inevitably follow. Kyle Haselden points out the inherent peril in letting the pew rule the pulpit until the pastor becomes only a paid special speaker. People will respect our high calling in Jesus Christ only if preachers respect it themselves, he observes.[7] Congregational sheep are generally willing to be led if the shepherd is ready to lead.

CREATIVE LEADERSHIP

There is no such term as *status quo* in the vocabulary of a truly New Testament church. Therefore, leadership must involve more than just caretaking. In his excellent book *Spiritual Leadership,* J. Oswald Sanders states the case in these words, "Some have more gift for conserving gains than for initiating new ventures . . . The true leader must have venturesomeness as well as vision."[8] Achieving churches are the result of imaginative pastoral direction. Most lay leaders will respond enthusiastically to fresh, creative programs and procedures. This does not mean that every church is ready for extensive overhauling immediately. Dr. A. E. Sanner, veteran district superintendent, wisely counseled that two major changes might be a safe limit in one's first year, or else the third change could be the pastor. However, variety adds spice to church life, and the majority of the flock will welcome variations from their customary practices.

Only a very small percentage of ministers is gifted with the ability to innovate. All too many could spend a week in a think tank and come out with nothing more than a headache. But every pastor can be an imitator. There are very few copyrights in the Kingdom. Wise pastors who sense their limitations in creativity will become successful borrowers. Denominational headquarters and publishing houses make available a continual supply of practical materials on church programming and promotion. Wide-awake boards provide their pastors with travel allowances so that they can visit pacesetting churches, counsel with their ministers, and bring home ideas and plans that can be adapted to their needs.

There may be a variety of excuses but there are no real reasons for churches to exist in a near fatal state of lethargy and sheer boredom. Any pastor can have access to methods and materials that will awaken the sleepiest saints and spark a surge of new vitality in the most lifeless congregation.

MINISTERIAL MOTIVATION

Church growth and achievement begins not with better-laid plans but with better-motivated people. And this starts with the shepherd-leader. Periodically the man or woman of God should give attention to his or her basic motivation.

Because their wage negotiations had broken off, the pilots of one of the major airlines instituted what they termed the W.O.E. program. These letters stood for "Withdrawal of Enthusiasm." Passengers were met by a sustained silence from the cockpit. There was no "Welcome Aboard!" No announcement was made of ground speed, altitude, or projected arrival time. No travelogue was given. Only the basic services were supplied.

When the ministry becomes just a matter of minimums and all enthusiasm has been withdrawn, the matter of incentives should be carefully examined. In Peter's treatise on pastoral practice referred to earlier, he admonishes that care of the flock should not be monetarily motivated—"not for filthy lucre" (1 Pet. 5:2). The minister's support is a legitimate responsibility of the church. Bishop Gerald Kennedy once stated that the poorest bargain in the world is an underpaid preacher. But by the same token, better salaries do not guarantee better ministers. The pay will never be good enough if we are just working for wages. However, pastors who are properly motivated and see the work of the Kingdom prosper will in turn find that their congregations are better able and more willing to increase their salaries.

It is even more necessary that there be proper and adequate motivation when church operations are not producing visible results. At best there will be some low ebbs in this enterprise. Whitlock describes the successful minister as "the kind of person who can encounter frustration and temporary failure and be able to rebound rather than capitulate to defeat."[9] Such fortitude is an absolute necessity. But what fuels this ability to bounce back? How can one maintain the dynamic enthusiasm so imperative in effective leadership?

The apostle provides the authoritative answer when he identifies the only adequate motivation in these words: "Because you are eager to serve the Lord" (1 Pet. 5:2, TLB). There is no other expedient. We are not serving the superintendent—either district or general. Our service stewardship is *through* the church, not *to* it. We *do it for Jesus' sake!* And that imparts a kind of glory to even the most mundane tasks. Here is the source of the eagerness to serve that lifts our ministry above minimums. This is the secret of maintaining the necessary romance in our vocation. It was love slavery at the beginning. It must always be so. There is a constancy about this motivation that is impervious to changing circumstances and fluctuating emotions. It will endure when all secondary incentives are exhausted.

THE MINISTER AS MOTIVATOR

This basic personal motivation equips one in turn to be an effective motivator. A layperson's service must be elevated from *have to* to *want to*. Duty is good but not good enough. If not raised to a higher motivational plane, it will almost invariably devolve into drudgery. No other shepherding skill is more pivotal than that of being able to lift the incentive level of the sheep.

Dr. Richard Le Tourneau, in *Management Plus*, writes:

> Motivation cannot be created simply by following a set of rules or conditions. . . . Motivation is a characteristic which develops spontaneously when the proper conditions, circumstances, and attitudes are present. One of the main conditions or attitudes that contributes to this motivation is the enthusiasm and drive of you, the manager.[10]

Essentially, *motivation is a person, not a method*. It can be caught better than taught. And it is more contagious than measles. Don't apologize for asking your people to "follow the leader" in this regard. Paul didn't. In dealing with the problem church at Corinth, which had among its other needs a lack of understanding of proper motivation, he went so far as to say, "Follow my example as I follow Christ's" (1 Cor. 11:1, NEB). This involved more than just the fact of following. Here was a selfless challenge to emulate the ardor and single-minded devotion with which he served his Lord.

Listen to Eisenhower's words again, "Leadership with *inexhaustible . . . energy to spur the efforts of lesser men*" (italics added). This is the public demonstration of that inner motivation. How do I energize others? By being more energetic myself. How do I get others to work harder? By working harder myself. Don't expect to follow Christ at a snail's pace and expect your people to sprint. Too many ministers find genuine renewal at a convention or retreat and then just come home and talk about it. As soon as the glow wears off, it's "business as usual." Small wonder that congregations don't get excited. They're waiting to see the difference demonstrated. A new evangelistic zeal in the pulpit. A fresh passion for personal soul winning. A driving concern that makes pastoral calling more than perfunctory and sets a pattern for lay visitation.

Another key to effective motivation is the leader's "creditability." There is no way to estimate the amount of good that could be done if no thought were given to who would receive the credit for it. LeTourneau comments:

> The ultimate degree to which you can motivate people to action . . . involves taking an idea . . . and then convincing your co-worker . . . that it is his idea, not yours. He will become very enthusiastic about something he feels is his idea because he has identified with it. . . . You should be more interested in getting the job done than in getting credit for it.[11]

This selfless strategy is another evidence of exemplary leadership motivation.

LIKE SHEPHERD, LIKE SHEEP

Someone has wisely observed that every great institution is the lengthening shadow of a great person. This truth has a universal application. Eisenhower in his discussion of leadership comments, "You can judge a . . . unit merely by knowing its commander. . . . The exact level of a commander's personality and ability is always reflected in his unit."[12]

What a frightening responsibility rests upon the pastor (commander). His church will be an accurate copy of its leader. No other human influence will be as formative. In the words of the plaque that President Harry S. Truman kept on his desk, "The buck stops here!" It cannot be passed on to anyone else.

But what a challenging opportunity. By precept and example the godly shepherd can reproduce an exemplary godliness in the flock. His faithful discipleship will be mirrored in theirs. His ethical patterns will become theirs. Through shared concerns for this common cause they will be welded together in a spiritual union until "the commander and the unit are almost one and the same thing."[13] This battle-ready army is now prepared to wage aggressive warfare for its Commander in Chief.

THE LIFESTYLE OF THE SHEPHERD

T. Harwood Pattison, in his classic text on pastoral theology *For the Work of the Ministry,* discusses at length the qualities that comprise what we will call "ministerial maturity":

> This quality . . . should run through all our nature: through our moral nature, saving us from the petty insolence of office and from slavish fear of others; through our intellectual nature, delivering us from undue subservience either to tradition or to current opinion; through our social nature, making us superior to fashion and class distinction; through our physical nature, teaching us self-denial, bravery, and endurance.[14]

Paul echoes this basic emphasis upon the character and resulting characteristics of the shepherd-overseer in the First Timothy passage quoted above. The personal and private aspects of the parson's life become every bit as determinative of success in shepherding as one's public ministry, for it is this setting that one's lifestyle will be molded. What one is and does behind the closed doors and drawn blinds of the study and parsonage, and in social and recreational activities, primarily conditions this "ministerial maturity."

Since by the very nature of the vocation, the minister is a public person, serious attention must be given to the cultivation of this private sector of life, or else it will be victimized by the never-ending official demands upon one's time. To ascertain whether there is a proper balance, it would be wise for one to keep a record of the time involved in the various activities that make up his life for a three-month or even better a six-month period. The day's record should be entered in a ledger either the last thing at night or the first thing the next morning. At the end of the recording period the totals will give an accurate reading on whether there is a significant imbalance in one's schedule.

The basic categories of such a study should be:

1. Official public ___ hours (total of the following)
    a. Preaching and teaching ___ hours
    b. Calling and personal evangelism ___ hours
    c. Counseling ___ hours
    d. Administration (office work, board and committee meetings) ___ hours
    e. Denominational (assemblies, boards, camps) ___ hours
    f. Community ___ hours
2. Official private ___ hours (total of the following)
    a. Sermon study and preparation ___ hours
    b. College or graduate study ___ hours
    c. Other study and preparation ___ hours
3. Personal ___ hours (total of the following)
    a. Private devotions ___ hours
    b. Business (banking, shopping) ___ hours
    c. Maintenance (parsonage, car) ___ hours
    d. Recreation (alone or with associates) ___ hours
    e. Recreation and social with spouse ___ hours
    f. Recreation and social with family ___ hours
    g. Time at home with family ___ hours

Pastor, disciplining yourself to make this time study is the first step. The next is honestly to face the results. The schedule should be a servant, not a master. If it needs to be changed, change it! This could make all the difference in your world. Speaking of the minister who has lost the romance of service, Dr. Stevenson comments:

> He is uninspired because he is undisciplined. . . . The key to the problem, then, seems to lie in setting up priorities and "redeeming the time." In practical terms this means "chaptering" each month and each week and plotting the course of each day. . . . What we need is an appointment book which will include not only public commitments but a number of private appointments.[15]

If one's *devotional life* has been neglected, it should be inserted in the schedule ahead of other responsibilities. In her biography of her renowned minister-husband, Mrs. Samuel Shoemaker recalls: "He believed that all clergy should really begin with a rule of life that included at least a half hour of personal devotion at the beginning of the day, and he felt that all discipline started there and succeeded or failed there."[16]

If there are indications that administration or calling have crowded in on one's *study schedule,* remedial action must be taken. Just as deadly is the practice of frittering away time in the study in casual reading or on the telephone. Dr. J. H. Jowett in his Yale Lectures on "The Preacher: His Life and Work" makes this pertinent observation, "If the study is a lounge, the pulpit will be an impertinence. It is, therefore, imperative that the preacher go into his study to do hard work."[17] Even the most eloquent preacher cannot consistently minister to the spiritual needs of his congregation without a carefully structured study program. Laypersons who work hard to be productive in their various vocations have a right to expect their pastor to do the same, even though there is no time clock to punch at the church or no daily production accounting to give. Lacking these mechanical motivators, ministers must be self-starters who rely on a strong sense of commitment to these serious responsibilities of shepherding to keep them consistent in their study habits.

After one has reserved an adequate block of time for study, he must arrange a schedule for *administrative work and counseling.* Since the morning is prime time for sermon preparation, some afternoon periods should be scheduled for these other duties as well as calling. These words that grace many pastors' studies beautifully define the scope of service that the shepherd renders from the study:

> *The pastor's study is a symbol of the calling of the Christian minister to be the shepherd of a flock of God. Here sermons are prepared to feed the congregation on God's Word. Here, the work of the church is planned so that the congregation may grow in grace and bear fruit in service, fellowship, teaching, and witnessing. Here you will always find a friend and a counselor in time of need. He will not be surprised at your sins, nor will he judge you in them, but he always invites you to share with him the wisdom and love of God, the knowledge of forgiveness of sins, and the saving grace of God in Christ Jesus, our Lord.*

RECREATION AND FAMILY LIFE

Four centuries ago Miguel de Cervantes observed that "the bow cannot always stay bent, nor can human frailty subsist without some lawful recreation." The demands of pastoral ministry are never-ending. The conscientious shepherd can work 16 hours a day, 7 days a week and never get everything done. But the commandment of God is very clear: "Six days shalt thou labour and do all thy work." While the Sabbath is a day of worship for both minister and laypersons, it is not a day of rest for the pastor. Failure to take a day off each week compromises the divine provision for the re-creation of one's physical, mental, and emotional being just as failure to observe the Sabbath robs one of spiritual renewal. Dr. Daniel Blain, psychiatrist and minister's son, advises: "The minister will seek to establish an adequate program of recreation, refreshment, and replenishment which will serve to restore his energies and nourish his mind and spirit. . . . High creativity seems to depend upon these fallow periods."[18]

Outdoor exercise or regular workouts should have a place on the pastor's weekly calendar just as much as any other ministerial activity. *It is not an option!* The rest of the week's work will not be done at full efficiency without it. And the length of one's ministry will be prolonged because of it.

Often such recreation can be made to serve a dual purpose by engaging in these activities with those whom you are seeking to win to the Lord. Cultivation of these contacts in this way is an invaluable aid to evangelism. Also, new converts can be strengthened by this fellowship. Many new Christians face a real adjustment in breaking the old patterns of sinful associations and activities, and these hours spent in wholesome recreation with their pastor will help immeasurably in this process.

Some pastors find Monday to be the best day to take off. Winding down from the strenuous schedule of Sunday and getting wound up for the week's work come naturally on this day. Others prefer to immediately follow up Sunday's visitors and take the flowers from the church to the sick, waiting until Tuesday for their own relaxation. Still others take a half day early in the week and then a half day on Saturday. But in this last case caution must be exercised that this privilege is not abused and the end result is two days off instead of one.

Pastors' spouses need recreation too. Perhaps the parsonage pressures have taken as much toll of their resources as the pulpit pressures have of their spouses'. They need to get away too. There is no law against including them in the plans for the day off. Baby-sitters can be secured. These elect spouses deserve this consideration, and the therapy of shared relaxation will do wonders for them.

Then, *what about the kids?* Too many of us try to salve our consciences by planning one or two weeks of vacation together. This is good, but it isn't good enough. Between Dad's or Mom's church activities and their school schedules it isn't easy to plan regular times together. But *daily family devotions are a must.* Breakfast time is probably the most practical time for most parsonage families. When the children are small, the reading of Bible stories will make the family altar interesting and contributive to their young lives. As they grow older, a varied menu of Bible readings from modern translations interspersed with selections from good devotional books will provide the spiritual strength that teenagers will sorely need as they go out to face the pressures of an unchristian society.

TIME SHOULD BE TAKEN FOR SOCIAL AND RECREATIONAL ACTIVITIES THAT CAN BE ENJOYED TOGETHER.

Charles M. Sheldon, the author of the Christian classic *In His Steps,* testifies that when he went away to university as an 18-year-old freshman, he was invited to join some questionable activity in the dormitory. Peer pressure was strong. He was about to yield when the Lord brought to his memory the sound of his father's voice praying for him at the family altar. He excused himself, went to his room, and made vows to God that were never broken. If we are too busy for family devotions, we are too busy!

In addition to this spiritual sharing, time should be taken for *social and recreational activities that can be enjoyed together.* It could even be on the printed calendar of the week in the church bulletin. No board meetings or other activities are to be scheduled on that night. Families are urged to spend the evening together. Children (as well as spouses) enjoy eating out. If it's nothing more than hamburgers and milkshakes, it's an event. Then come home and play games or engage in some other activities the family enjoys doing together.

> PARSONAGES MAY NOT BE PALACES, BUT HAPPY MEMORIES OF GOOD TIMES SHARED THERE WILL ENDOW PREACHERS' KIDS WITH A TREASURE FAR GREATER THAN A KING'S BOUNTY.

Preacher-dads or moms should not be too busy to attend musical or athletic events at school when their boys and girls are participating. And at least some Saturdays should be dedicated to outings that the whole family can enjoy. All too quickly these youngsters are grown and gone, and pastors who have been too busy to take time for family fun and fellowship can never reclaim these priceless opportunities. In the final analysis, what shall it profit a minister if he gain the whole ecclesiastical world and lose his own children? Parsonages may not be palaces, but happy memories of good times shared there will endow preachers' kids with a treasure far greater than a king's bounty. There bonds of affection will be forged that will tie them to God and the church.

The social life of the shepherd may be classified somewhere between business and pleasure. A large part of it will be spent in the company of parishioners. An invitation to dinner in a member's home provides an excellent opportunity for both recreation and shepherding. Attendance at Sunday School class and youth group socials should be accepted as both privilege and responsibility.

If such socializing does not come naturally, it should be cultivated. Both the shepherd and the sheep need this informal, relaxed social contact. Then, on occasion the doors of the parsonage should be opened for fellowship. Jay Adams declares: "Every minister . . . must be 'given to hospitality' (Titus 1:8) . . . Hospitality in the Christian community is so important that two New Testament books were written to discuss the subject (2 and 3 John)."[19]

Some pastors entertain the members of the church board and their spouses each year. Others plan to have a reception for new members in the manse following the Sunday night service on the day they are received.

These social occasions weld the lives of pastor and people together as nothing else can. Caution should be exercised that they encompass the largest segment of the congregation possible. Nothing will destroy a shepherd's effectiveness more quickly than social favoritism. While it is only natural that there are certain people whom we enjoy being with more than others, *exclusive friend-ships must be conscientiously avoided!*

These activities also present an opportunity for the shepherd to be an exem-plar of the social graces for the flock. Little things do matter. Such things as a husband opening the car door for his wife are important. These little courtesies speak volumes to the members of the congregation who look to their leaders for a pattern of deportment. Many laypersons do not have the benefit of training in these amenities. If they ever learn the rudiments of gracious living, it will be as they observe the example of their minister. On the other hand, failure to perform these little niceties will be interpreted as a lack of respect for one's spouse by those who know the essentials of social decorum. Carelessness at this point may lead to an erosion of the confidence of such flock members in their shepherd.

THE SHEPHERD'S SUPPORT

Ministers' salaries being what they are (the lowest of all professions) and liv-ing costs being what they are (higher than ever), making ends meet takes some doing. While Protestant ministers are not required to take a formal vow of poverty, in effect when one enters the ministry this is part of the commitment. Relatively few churches can pay salaries equivalent to what plumbers or brick-layers make, to say nothing of physicians or bankers. And construction workers don't invest the high cost of up to seven years of higher education in preparation for their trade. Neither do they have to wear dress clothes to work or drive their cars as much as 30,000 miles a year to serve their clientele. At the same time, ministers will not be organizing group pressure to better themselves financially.

The only possible answer is a *selfless commitment to live within one's ministerial means*. God honors the faith of His servants who will dare to put this principle to the test. And the same God will honor the efforts of district superintendents who evidence concern for their pastors' welfare by systematically reminding church boards that their (shepherd) laborers are worthy of their (best possible) hire.

Ministerial ethics plus good common sense may make it difficult for a pastor to broach the subject of his support to the church board. However, more and more districts are recommending that *this matter be considered as a routine item at least annually and preferably semiannually.* The chairman of the finance committee should be reminded by the district superintendent or the church secretary to put this subject on the agenda. By all means it should be discussed at the time the budget for the coming church year is being prepared. Then, cost-of-living and merit increases may well be considered halfway through the year.

A few churches have experimented with incentive salary increases based upon such indicators as membership, Sunday School, and financial growth. This system has some obvious pitfalls, but it does highlight the principle that nonproducing pastors should not expect the same salary raises that their achieving colleagues receive. It is hard to convince a church board composed of business professionals who compete in the marketplace for their income that their pastor should be given a substantial increase in remuneration when there are few if any new members to help provide this additional revenue. And if the financial report indicates that receipts are not up significantly, how can a budget justify a sizable salary raise?

The parable of the talents teaches two timeless lessons. First, that *increase deserves reward,* and second, that *it is possible to be good, but good for nothing!* The one-talent servant was not accused of being crooked. His wickedness was directly linked to his slothfulness. Certainly good shepherds have higher motivation than the monetary; but in the divine economy as in the human, diligence and exceptional service will not go unrewarded.

Dr. W. T. Purkiser makes this wise comment on the minister's money matters: "The pastor's own finances are of utmost importance. He may find himself faced with the necessity of living and looking like a professional . . . on less than the income of a day laborer. But unless his income equals his outgo, his upkeep will be his downfall!"[20]

THE FAMILY BUDGET

Since the pastor's support will always be limited, serious attention must be given to the management of personal finances. This begins with careful record keeping. Part of the necessity for this is related to accurate tax reporting. In his excellent book *Money Management for Ministers,* Manfred Holck advises:

> The clergyman who fails to keep adequate records to support his income tax calculations is asking for trouble. . . . You should keep a running record of car expenses, contributions to your church and other charitable organizations, taxes, interest you pay on loans and mortgages, all medical expenses and drugs, and professional expenses (books, supplies, entertainment).[21]

However, even those records are not sufficient. Just as the church must have a budget that anticipates both income and expenditure, so must the parsonage. Without it fiscal chaos can easily result.

Budget items for a pastor in a utilities-furnished parsonage should include the following:

- Food
- Furnishings and equipment
- Operations (sundry supplies and repairs)
- Clothing (and cleaning)
- Medical care
- Personal care (hair care, cosmetics)
- Tithes, offerings, and other contributions

- Taxes
- Reading and recreation
- Education
- Transportation (car payments, official and personal travel)
- Insurance
- Interest
- Savings
- Miscellaneous

Some of these are fixed items—taxes, tithe, insurance, and so forth. Others such as food, clothing, and medical care must be estimated. The total should be balanced against one's anticipated income. Then the budget should be checked monthly to see if it is being kept in balance; and, if necessary, certain restrictions should be imposed in areas that are getting out of hand.

One of the mortal enemies of a balanced budget is credit buying. More than one pastor has finally come to the place of burning the credit cards, and reverted to paying cash for all purchases. There is really no such thing as "easy payments"! How much wiser to institute a plan of *enforced savings* where up to 10 percent of one's income is deposited in a savings account. Then when sales on clothing, furniture, or appliances are advertised, paying cash will not only result in the benefit of the reduced price but also in saving the interest charged on installment payments. Some pastors follow this procedure in purchasing their cars and find that this results in hundreds of dollars of savings. This discipline pays big dividends.

But even the best-kept budget will get out of balance occasionally and necessitate the borrowing of money. A reasonable line of credit at a local bank can be a very present help in time of need. The acquaintance of an officer in the bank where you do business should be cultivated so that a loan can be secured when necessary. Prompt repayment and, if possible, prepayment will insure that your credit is good when you need it. *Finance companies should be studiously avoided.* Their exorbitant interest rates do not constitute even a last resort.

THE PARSONAGE

Traditionally churches have provided housing for their pastors. Too often this amenity is taken for granted by ministers. While it does not show as part of the cash income, the financial benefit of a utilities-furnished parsonage is considerable. The church supplies maintenance of the parsonage, including painting and repairs, and often puts in carpeting and even some items of furnishings. This can quickly add up to several thousand a year. The other side of the coin is that there are also advantages for the church in owning a parsonage. It builds equity in the house that provides a valuable asset on its balance sheet. Then, too, many states exempt churches from paying property taxes on parsonages, so this rather sizable amount of money is saved.

In recent years a growing number of pastors have indicated an interest in purchasing their own housing as a means of building equity toward retirement. There is some merit in this plan. Without the necessity of owning a home, too many ministers spend their total income and face their retired years without housing or funds with which to purchase it. Some of the *advantages* of owning one's own home are:

1. Owning property is an inducement for longer tenure. Unless one stays at least 10 years, most payments have gone toward interest and very little equity is built up.
2. The building up of financial equity, which is further enhanced when a rising economy appreciates the value of the property.
3. Property taxes and mortgage interest may be taken as tax deductions and are therefore not total losses.
4. The peace of mind in knowing that the preacher's kids are not abusing the church's property.

On the other hand there are some definite *disadvantages* to this policy.

1. Few pastors have accumulated enough savings for a down payment and consequently must face the added financial load of a second mortgage.
2. Too many churches cannot or will not pay a housing allowance sufficient to enable a pastor to buy a house adequate for pastoral entertaining responsibilities.
3. The pastor must pay property taxes that the church often need not pay, and many church boards are reluctant to add this amount to a housing allowance.
4. The pastor must bear the total cost of furnishing and maintaining the house.
5. In a depressed economy the pastor may have difficulty selling the property when moving, and may take a sizable financial loss on the transaction.
6. Owning property may tend to make a pastor stay longer than he should.

Among those who have had experience with both procedures the consensus seems to be that in many cases the church-owned parsonage proves to be of greater advantage to all concerned.

PROVIDING FOR THE FUTURE

Certainly it is the part of wisdom to make reasonable provision for the tomorrows. This should begin with an *adequate insurance program*. With the extremely high cost of medical care it is imperative that the pastor's family be covered with *health insurance*. Many churches have written this into their budgets, but if necessary the pastor should pay the premiums. One major hospital bill can bring financial disaster to the parsonage if there is no insurance coverage. Then, very early in ministry, every pastor should begin investing in *life insurance*. John C. Banker counsels: "Along with a savings account there should be a sound scheme of insurance equal to at least two or three years' salary to protect the family in the event of the death of the breadwinner."[22] A good insurance agent can design a program of both decreasing term and endowment insurance, which will provide maximum security for the family during the years when the children are at home.

During the period beginning at age 50 and continuing up to retirement, the pastor should give maximum attention to laying aside funds for the time when his ministerial income will cease. *Social Security* benefits coupled with the basic *pension program* of the church should provide "bread and butter" support. Additional *money-purchase pension* and *tax-sheltered annuities* will lift this minimum to a more livable level. With the children educated, more money should be available for these supplemental programs. *Savings* invested in government securities, banks, savings and loan institutions, and credit unions are generally very safe.

Investments in *real estate* can pose problems. Unless one has a competent agent to manage rentals, they can take a great deal of time and attention that no pastor has to spare. However, if a pastor is certain where he wishes to retire, the purchase of a home that can be rented in the meantime to make the payments has some merit. There is a question whether many ministers should invest in the *stock market.* Two safeguards should be employed if one invests in equities:

1. Don't buy stocks and bonds with funds you cannot afford to lose and *never with borrowed money.*

2. Seek qualified, professional counsel before purchasing equities.

Last, but not least, *make a will!* Young pastors and their spouses as well as older ones dare not neglect this matter. Even if one does not have sizable assets, a will is absolutely necessary so that in case of a tragedy the legal guardians for minor children will be officially appointed. Without this the court may assign them to unchristian homes that stand for the exact opposite of what their parents believed. The services of a well-recommended attorney in the state where you are presently residing should be secured. Since the statutes of states differ widely, it is wise to have wills redrawn when you move to a new state. And both husband and wife should have wills. These should be kept in a safe deposit box with other important papers. It is well to have the signature of a close relative authorized for entry to the box so that insurance policies and other documents can be secured in case of emergency.

---

1. Dwight D. Eisenhower, *At Ease* (New York: Doubleday and Co., 1967), 254.

2. Vance Havner, *Living in Kingdom Come* (Westwood, N.J.: Fleming H. Revell Co., 1967), 12.

3. Ibid., 28-29.

4. Lawrence O. Richards, *A New Face for the Church* (Grand Rapids: Zondervan Publishing House, 1970), 118.

5. David A. Redding, *What Is the Man?* (Waco, Tex.: Word Books, 1970), 21.

6. Dag Hammarskjöld, *Markings,* trans. Leif Sjöberg and W. H. Auden (New York: Alfred A. Knopf, 1964), 105.

7. Kyle Haselden, *The Urgency of Preaching* (New York: Harper and Row, 1963), 106-7.

8. John Oswald Sanders, *Spiritual Leadership* (Chicago: Moody Press, 1967), 116.

9. Glenn E. Whitlock, *From Call to Service* (Philadelphia: Westminster Press, 1968), 88.

10. Richard LeTourneau, *Management Plus* (Grand Rapids: Zondervan Publishing House, 1973), 64.

11. Ibid., 84-85.

12. Eisenhower, *At Ease,* 253.

13. T. Harwood Pattison, *For the Work of the Ministry* (Philadelphia: American Baptist Publication Society, 1907), 26.

14. Ibid.

15. Dwight E. Stevenson, *The False Prophet* (New York: Abingdon Press, 1965), 91.

16. Helen (Smith) Shoemaker, *I Stand by the Door: The Life of Sam Shoemaker* (New York: Harper and Row, 1967), 117.

17. John H. Jowett, *The Preacher, His Life and Work* (New York: George H. Doran Co., 1912), 114.

18. W. T. Purkiser, *The New Testament Image of the Ministry* (Kansas City: Beacon Hill Press of Kansas City, 1969), 132.

19. Jay C. Adams, *Shepherding God's Flock* (Philadelphia: Presbyterian and Reformed Publishing Co., 1975), 35.

20. Purkiser, *New Testament Image,* 130.

21. Manfred Holck, *Money Management for Ministers* (Minneapolis: Augsburg Press, 1966), 32-33.

22. John C. Banker, *Personal Finance for Ministers* (Philadelphia: Westminster Press, 1968), 10.

Adapted from chapters 3 and 13 of *The Ministry of Shepherding: A Study of Pastoral Practice* (Kansas City: Beacon Hill Press of Kansas City, 1976), 32-39, 185-99.

I never remember in all my
Christian course, a period now
of sixty-nine years and four months,
that I ever sincerely and patiently
sought to know the will of God
by the teaching of the Holy Ghost,
through the instrumentality of
the Word of God, but I have always
been directed rightly.

—George Müller

Quoted in *Christian: Commit Yourself!* Paul S. Rees (Westwood, N.J.: Fleming H. Revell Company, 1957), 81.

7

THE LIFELONG ADVENTURE OF PARTNERSHIP WITH GOD

Milo L. Arnold

THOUGH A MINISTER lives many years and rejoices in them all, he still will have to accept the fact that he must leave his task unfinished and his field partially unexplored. The minister walks toward an edgeless horizon. Always he presses toward the place where the sky meets the earth, only to find that, when he reaches the apparent edge, there is another wide expanse beyond. There are always distant hills between him and the fulfillment of his eager quest. Instead of his work being completed by the accomplishment of a given task, it is enlarged. Each task he does widens his field and increases the circumference of his influence. As his contact with need is increased, each completed project exposes him to many more waiting areas of service.

A pastor may look upon the ministry during his first years as a task to fulfill, but the eagerness of a devout pastor will lead him to discover the endlessness of his duty. There is no place to quit until somewhere along the unending furrow he will fall and God shall see that he has done his duty. He will not have finished the field. There is no community so small but that there is more work than a pastor can do and none so large but that a pastor may fulfill the will and demand of God for him.

A minister must have an insatiable curiosity. If he does not, he will never plumb the depth of the vocation nor adventure into the far reaches of his field. There are those who say that a minister loses his effectiveness after he reaches a given age, but it would be better to say he loses his effectiveness when he ceases to wonder. In fact some pastors, being unable to follow a holy inquisitiveness, have discovered that the ministry was no place for them. The minister who becomes content with what he has discovered of truth will starve both himself and those who look to him for spiritual food. No wonder Paul kept useful to the last, for he willfully drove himself through the years, saying, "That I may know him." His motto might have been, "I press." For Paul there was not only a new field for evangelism over the next hill but a new discovery of God in the next waiting experience.

The Galilean fishermen began a continuing adventure when they left their nets to follow the Lord, who said He would make them "fishers of men." Their preparation to serve and their being made into fishers of men was a project that never ended. To their very deaths they were learning new things about life, and in the hour of dying pushed back the curtain to stand in awe and wonder at the things God has prepared for them that love Him. They learned a lot but they didn't learn it all. They discovered a grand expanse of living but knew that beyond the next rise were new worlds to explore.

The minister's preparation is never finished and provides a continuing adventure in becoming. When he has finished his schooling and enters for the first time into his pulpit with a crisp diploma, a well-prepared sermon, and a bright vision of his future, he suddenly discovers that he is not prepared. He must learn more and more. Each week the needs of life swallow his supplies in hasty gulps and he must attend his preparing lest he stand before his people with his supply exhausted. He finds his life constantly too small and his knowledge inadequate.

He soon must learn that, though he minister for many years, the supply is never enough. He never knows enough nor has he an adequate bounty to set before his people. There must be new books read and new skills developed. There must be greater effectiveness and stronger sinews of soul. When he learns one new truth, he knows the exhilarating adventure of putting it to work, only to find that for the next assignment he must adventure again into a hitherto undeveloped area.

The minister must experience a constant adventure in expanding his own vision. There are those whose small vision is easily realized and who see beyond it nothing much more to accomplish. They will live but briefly in the ministry. He who would follow the Christ in a dedicated adventure will find his vision continually extending. It will project itself to something new and exciting from each fresh vista. He has the ability to see more and bigger things to do. He will never arrive. Jesus did not go to Calvary because He was through with all the things He could see to do. He went because His time was come and He saw there something bigger to do than He had done before. He could have continued from then until now with His ministry of healing and teaching without arriving at a finished task. But He was challenged by a greater task that could be done only by the giving of His very all on the Cross of atonement. Easter morning found Him still eager to keep new appointments, to do new things, and to make new plans. His rising from Mount Olivet was charged with His glowing words, "I go to prepare a place and I will come again."

One evening at a wedding reception a bridegroom and bride were chatting with me when he turned to her and remarked, "Honey, look me over carefully tonight, for you'll never see me look this good again." I waited until I could speak to him alone and challenged what he had said. I reminded him that if he allowed what he said to be true he was being unfair. He should look better than this many times. He owed it to his wife to make her as proud on many occasions as she was the night she was his bride. Every man should improve his appearance, his culture, his grooming, and his graces with the passing years. The man who looks upon his wedding night as the high noon of his attractiveness is being shortsighted.

> **THE MINISTER WHO HAS ARRIVED AT HIS BEST HAS STOPPED TOO SOON.**

The minister who has arrived at his best has stopped too soon. He should never arrive. He should keep climbing to his dying day. We recognize the human limitations and the contrast attrition of years upon the body, but the servant of God should be more gracious, more charming, more lovable, and more personable as time goes on. Remember, the inner person is renewed day by day. It is too bad when any minister begins to look behind him to his greatest day. The greatest day should be ahead.

It is true that a minister may need to accept smaller pastorates and may serve in less conspicuous positions in his ecclesiastical setting, but the minister should still be climbing. His vision for accomplishment must become ever sharper, his ambition to glorify God more eager, and his quest for learning better methods of doing his new duties more demanding.

Occasionally a minister is tempted to believe he has pushed back the boundaries of his parish to the limit. He feels that he cannot accomplish more under the limitations of the community. He may think he has reached all of the people who are reachable by his church in that particular field. It may be true that some communities do not offer a very large field so far as the number of persons within reach are concerned; but let no minister think he has accomplished all of the task so long as he is dealing with people and God. Even if there were only five people in the area and a minister had led them all to God, he could still spend a lifetime in making them more godly. He could have many years there and still never fully accomplish a completed ministry. Our horizon is not bounded merely by the edge of a community but by the possibilities of each person. Each new experience of Christian culture into which we lead an individual exposes him to the possibility of another and loftier one. Each lesson our members learn makes it possible for them to master a more advanced one. Each enrichment that strengthens a life opens up a new door of growth.

The horizons of a minister's work are never reached. When you go as far as you can see now, you will find that the sky meets the earth yet a long way off. There may be areas where the world looks small and the task limited, but before you get to the edge of it you find that it is not there.

There is no limit to the land a minister can possess in his own preparation, in his undertakings for God, in his service to others, and in his life fulfillment.

Our task is always being opened to new exposures by the changing needs of our world, the changing fortunes of our people, and new doors opened by new days. If we are too inclined to want to move to bigger fields, get appointments to larger churches, or ask for wider expanses, it is likely that we have never discovered the real breadth of our present parish. A minister might keep moving to a larger city and still be smothered by narrow horizons. A pastor who finds his horizons hedged in is in need of a new vision. Some of God's most effective men and women have served churches in small communities. They have learned to make a much fuller investment in a few people rather than a limited imprint upon many. Some farmers make more money from a small farm that they till with care than others make on a large farm that they work carelessly. It is always possible that the Lord and the church officials may ask a minister to move to a more promising field, but no minister should need to move because there is not enough opportunity to challenge his soul where he is. The minister who sees nothing to do just isn't seeing with eyes kindled by dedication to God and humanity.

In the ministry there is always room further up. The opportunity for advancement is limitless. Our difficulty arises when we allow our ambitions to become either perverted or weak. Some ministers will see a gold mine in communities where others can't even find a colorful stone. Some ministers will find a staggering opportunity where others say there is nothing to challenge them. The true minister sees a beckoning, ever-receding horizon and is thrilled.

THE ADVENTURE OF A SHARED SELF

The value of an oil field is not in how much oil is stored under the ground but in how much is recoverable. Even so, the value of a minister is not in how much potential he has but in how much of him can be expressed in impact upon the lives of others. A minister's measure of usefulness is fixed by what he can give, not by what he possesses. The most brilliant sermons are not always the most helpful. The best-trained counselors are not always the most effective in consultation. The ablest administrator is not invariably the best pastor.

A minister is measured not only by what he has to give but also by how able he is in giving it. Jesus admonished His disciples that the path to greatness was through service, and the secret of getting the real adventure out of living was in giving themselves away effectively. The pastor who fails to follow this admonition is destined to disappointment in his office as a Christian minister. Self-giving is the essence of ministering.

For over 38 years it has been my privilege to live among the group of great men and women known as the ministers of Christ. They have been splendid persons. They have been of different denominations, different creeds, and varied practices. Some have been highly trained and others poorly trained, some graceful and others crude. They have possessed varying degrees of effectiveness. Among these ministers have been some whose lives were a splendid adventure. They have lived and worked as ministers who found excitement and interest in their work. They were eager in their assignments and well-rewarded in the finer values of life. There have been other ministers who showed no spirit of adventure, no zest for living, and no riches of abundant inner reward.

SOME MINISTERS WHO HAVE BEEN UNQUESTIONABLY DEDICATED TO GOD WERE WOEFULLY UNABLE TO GIVE THEMSELVES TO PEOPLE.

Watching these ministers, I have observed that their effectiveness in changing the lives of others bore a relationship to their sense of inner reward. However, not only were these factors related to each other, but both aspects were geared to the minister's ability to share himself with others. The ministers who were unable to project themselves unselfishly into the lives of others were both unhappy and ineffectual. The ministers whose unselfishness was genuine and whose lives were projected best were both happy and successful. Some ministers who have been unquestionably dedicated to God were woefully unable to give themselves to people.

The ability of self-sharing is in great measure developed in early childhood and is influenced by the attitudes of parents. Because of this, many persons find it easy to be outgoing in adult life while others find it difficult. Persons who in childhood were trained to be defensive will need a great measure of divine grace and human effort to overcome their handicap. It can be done, however, and every person who serves God, either in the ministry or as a layperson, will find it necessary to cultivate the ability for self-giving. The ablest preacher can give the people no more in his sermon than he can give of himself.

The past decades have brought great changes to the minister's community image and the responsibility of the clergy. For some years there was a marked ascendancy in both the demands made upon him and the dignity awarded him. The ministry became better trained, better equipped, and more highly professional. Doctors, psychiatrists, and educators included them as professional equals. But the growing demands upon their time and the increasing exposure of their situations caused many ministers to lose sight of their original purpose as servants of the people in the name of Jesus Christ.

In a world given to scientific test-tube examination, many ministers suddenly found themselves unable to live confidently. They had somewhat forsaken their former foundations in order to stand on the proud pedestal of professional acceptance and now that pedestal was no longer secure. Some became amateur psychiatrists, sociologists, counselors, or office personnel. Many of them adjusted their concept of God and their message to conform to the test tubes of science when neither the scientists nor the people asked it. Many gave up their faith in God as they had known God and began to live as though God were but a great, unexplainable, mysterious, imper-sonal force. Their faceless God became meaningless to them and their congregations. The ministry did not attract people, and the result was frustration. Empty churches, empty sermons, empty lives, and empty prayers gnawed their hearts out. Finally some began to rationalize their position by saying that God was dead anyway. They were but trying to help people find in their concept of God that which would solve the current evils of society rather than that which would change their hearts.

> THE MINISTER WITHOUT GOD HAS NO MORE TO GIVE THAN THE ATTORNEY, THE ENGINEER, OR THE DOCTOR.

The minister who seeks to give himself to people without having a God to offer them is giving so little that people will turn away in disgust. People want a minister to give them a to-tal self, enriched, enhanced, and fulfilled by the presence of God in his life. The minister without God has no more to give than the attorney, the engineer, or the doctor. The minister whose life is filled with the presence and grace of God has something to give. This unique gift will find a welcome place in the lives of many.

The minister who is able to give himself, together with the ministry of di-vine grace, is in demand. The adequacy of God in our lives is a prime essential.

New doors of usefulness await the minister with a deep personal relation-ship with God. The widening field of human need is great. The expanding pro-fessional field of the ministry provides added opportunity. Without a doubt, there will be a growing demand for the minister with a God-centered life. More and more people will turn to him for help in the very personal areas of life. But the minister of today must be on guard as never before lest he allow himself to deviate from basic Christian self-giving to mere professionalism. He must in-clude the ministry of counseling and guidance but without allowing himself to become other than a servant of Christ.

The bottleneck of the ministry is the hard fact that the minister cannot meet all the needs nor answer all the demands made upon him. Only as we maintain such a personal exposure to people as to enable us to openheartedly give ourselves to them can we serve them. The one who ministers must give himself as well as his services. All his talent, ability, and usefulness must be wrapped in his own person, which he gives out to his flock.

What an adventure Jesus Christ found in ministering. His very life was charged with eagerness. He did not work as one who was forced by an outer command but as one charged by an inner compulsion. He enjoyed His ministry because He was sharing himself. His eager life needed no prodding save the yearning to give himself away for the sake of others. He did not give merely His miracles. He gave himself. He did not stop with giving sermons or consolations. He gave himself. He did not stop when He rebuked a man, but He kept on until He gave himself. He did not give mere broken bread and poured-out wine; He poured out himself! He belonged to every person He touched, and every person who knew the comfort of His ministry knew the closeness of His beating heart. Could it be that we sometimes seek to give our sermons, our lectures, our consultations, and our services without the outpouring of ourselves?

The acceptance of the ministry as a profession rather than as a calling may tempt us to give less of ourselves. In the Early Church men and women entered the ministry at great personal cost. The very rigors attendant upon the life of the minister culled from its ranks all but the utterly dedicated. The only persons who got into the ministry were those who knew the inner self-crucifixion essential to the giving of themselves. They took up the office of minister because of a deep sense of being called. They prepared to lay down their lives rather than fail to follow the divine voice. With that kind of dedication it was natural for them to be drawn very close to the people whom they served and with whom they shared the hazards of Christian witnessing. The rapport between pastor and people was close because it often included the actual giving of their lives together. Ministers who had only skills to give were not willing to identify themselves with the ministry. Only ministers with self-abnegation would pay the price.

Today the pastor can perform the official functions of his office apart from the essential demands of self-giving. His living standard is as high as that of the average member of his congregation. In social status he is among the most accepted people of the community. His pulpit is protected by law and his freedom of speech guaranteed by the constitution. The ministry is now a very rewarding life and provides great satisfactions for ambitious persons. This is all very good and supplies great opportunity as long as ministers do not allow their incentives to change or their purposes to dissipate. It is not necessary that this pleasant situation should diminish a pastor's dedication, but it does make possible a continuance in office after dedication has ceased to motivate. The minister must be sure that he keeps himself on the altar after the things that helped keep his forebears there have been removed.

The tendency to specialization in the various fields of ministerial service may present a hazard to the self-giving of some ministers. Our medical sciences have made great strides in these days of specialized services and we welcome the progress thus gained; however, the doctors themselves will agree that not all is gain. The old family doctor was able to give some ministrations impossible to the specialist. He was a personal friend, a trusted neighbor, and a man close to the suffering heart of the community. He knew all of the family secrets and didn't tell them. He knew all the family's sins and didn't scorn the family. The specialist may know how to perform surgery on your heart, but he does not know how difficult you find it to get along with your mother-in-law. The highly trained specialist can repair a broken bone but does not know about the broken heart. The disappearance of the family doctor from the American scene brought a serious loss to the emotional security of many people.

THE SPECIALIST GIVES COUNSEL AND THERAPY, BUT THE BROKENHEARTED PEOPLE WANT A MINISTER WHO GIVES THEM HIS HEART.

The minister cannot know the full adventure of the ministry if he touches only specialized problems in the lives of his people. The specialist is good in his place, but he is too far removed from the lives of most people to render the service they need. If a minister allows his desire for specialization to remove him from the comfortable proximity with people, he has reduced rather than enlarged his effectiveness. A young minister came from his graduate studies well-trained in the field of counseling but was frustrated by the fact that nobody came to him for help. He had not yet learned that people do not share their personal lives with people who seem like strangers. People prefer a pastor who is close to them rather than a specialist who is afar off. The pastor must give himself. The specialist gives counsel and therapy, but the brokenhearted people want a minister who gives them his heart. Emotional proximity is more sought after than is specialized training. The minister who becomes a specialist in any one line must guard lest he give his techniques and not himself. The minister who knows enough to be a specialist but who is magnanimous enough to make no display of it will likely keep both his skill and his rapport with his people. The knowledge of special fields will help any minister render a fuller service, but being known as a specialist narrows his field too much for the pastorate. It is better to be known as a minister of the gospel while knowing and using the finest special skills. There is no reason why a pastor cannot be a counselor, a lecturer, a writer, or an expert in any one of many fields; but when he becomes identified as something other than a minister of the gospel, he loses his opportunity as a pastor. Some have even paid the price of remoteness from their people for the sake of being known as theologians.

The involvement of the minister of today in so many community tasks can prevent the fullest giving of himself in the area where the need is greatest. It is becoming easy for the minister to give himself to things rather than to people. In the days of our grandparents, the minister's field of responsibility was more narrowly defined than today. Now he must be business manager, public-relations spokesperson, television or radio personality, community leader, and helper in every kind of community enterprise. He must know the business of the church from its insurance matters to the kind of lawn seed to sow. He is expected to hold many threads and tangle none.

Through the years many fine people have come to my study to share their heartaches and problems, explaining that they were members of another church but their pastor was so busy that they were reluctant to bother him. Without a doubt their pastor would have been glad to weep with them and pray with them, but they felt too unimportant in his program. He was very busy. It is easy for the minister to make the mistake of mentioning how busy he is and advertising all of the things he does, so that people feel that seeking help for their problems would be an imposition. They give up their pastor to lesser things and find another way to bear their burdens.

No pastor should be too busy to make his people welcome when their loads are heavy. No pastor should impress his people with his busyness to the point that they feel he is out of their reach. This is a mistake too frequently made. No minister can pay his debt to people by giving himself to his church. When he loses sight of the persons whose heavy hearts need comforting, he has lost his real purpose in the ministry.

How can I give myself more fully? This is the question asked by every sincere minister of the gospel. There can be no better study than to go again to the paths of Jesus Christ and watch Him experience the surging adventure of self-sharing. He gave himself, not just His ministries. He gave himself to His enemies, refusing to destroy them to save himself, but allowing them to crucify Him in order that they might be saved. Can we learn from this?

Jesus did not allow himself to be contained by the busy machinations of the religious organization to the place where He was an impersonal leader. Rather, He kept close to the poor, the beggar, the lonely person, and the children. His greatest concern seemed to be for the need of the least important person. Can we learn from this?

He did not allow himself to be fettered by material offers nor bound by titles to property. He did not look to see which side of the bread was buttered nor where He might find the best meals. The size of the parsonage or the fame of the church would not have entered into His considerations, for He was giving himself. Can we learn from this?

He refused to be bound by the opinions of community leaders or influenced in His preaching by the people who could give the largest offerings. His message was never geared to the elite of the crowd, but He offered His hope to all who came—and His message was always the same. He did not shrink when confronted with a crown of thorns nor waver when a cross appeared. He was not out to escape hardship but to give himself. Can we learn from this?

Jesus was able to give so much of himself because He created a desire in the hearts of people to be the kind of person He was. These lessons we can well retain. We succeed in the measure in which we give ourselves. We cannot give more of ourselves than we ourselves become. People will not want what we have unless they see in us the kind of persons they want to become.

No minister continues to be a good pastor when he becomes more concerned about the size of his church than about the needs of his people. There is a deep sense of priesthood about the Christian ministry. We share many very personal matters of our people. Their sins, their failures, their hopes, and their aspirations are our business. We must represent God to the people in our sermons. For us to preach the demands of divine law without feeling the deep suffering of human failure will but add fear to their guilt and lead them into no reconciliation with God. Our Lord became both Priest and Sacrifice. We, as His followers in the ministry, must recognize the demand for self-sharing and present our bodies a living sacrifice to God on behalf of those to whom we minister. It is fine to build churches and pastor large parishes, but it is fundamental that we serve people and glorify God. The woman taken in the act of sin would never have been saved by the legalism of the synthetic priests who condemned her. Jesus did not diminish the force of the law that hung over her, but He did recognize the penitence and sorrow of the heart beating within her.

The people want the minister to be so close to their lives that he is thought of as part of the family. They like to know he is in town and will feel a measure of insecurity when he is away. They like to have him come near to them and share with them in all of the contingencies of their lives.

The people do not want a compromising minister nor will they respect a pastor who lowers the gospel demands for their personal convenience. They want a minister to be a true prophet of God, dealing honestly with them and pointing out their sins in bold accusation. To this he must give himself with fearless, reckless abandon. He must treat rich and poor alike and deal with sin in the same rugged terms wherever he finds it. He must never ask what returns he will get for being honest but will consider integrity as its own reward.

> THE HIGHEST-SOUNDING SERMON ON EARTH WILL MEAN NOTHING IF IT IS RELATED CHIEFLY TO PEOPLE WHO ARE ABSENT.

The minister must keep to his calling if he is to keep close to his people. He must be cautious about sharing himself with campaigns and reformations in the community political situation. He must not allow himself to become the mere voice of a campaigner nor be used as a pawn by people who have an axe to grind. His message must be geared to human need, filled with divine grace, and applied with personal ministrations. He must be so related to his calling that he talks about the sins the people commit, the problems the people experience, the hopes the people feel, and the dreams the people have. The highest-sounding sermon on earth will mean nothing if it is related chiefly to people who are absent.

The minister must remember that people will come for his sermons only when they come for him, and they will come for him only when they see in him some representation of God and of the persons they want to be. They will come wanting to be loved, for they are terribly lonely. They will come wanting to be healed, for they are badly bruised in spirit. They will come to him for rebuke, for they know they have fallen short. They will come for guidance, for they know not which way to turn. They will come yearning to be forgiven, for they are deeply penitent. They will come to the minister for all of these things because they know he is ready to give himself in the name of Christ.

When people come to the minister for a sermon, they do not seek so much a perfect delivery as a personal message that relates to them. They do not care to know much about how close the minister is to the great philosophers, but they want to know how close he can come to them. When they ask him to conduct a funeral for a loved one, they do not ask him because he knows the right forms so much as because they feel he knows them and their loneliness. When young people come to him for marriage they do not come just because of his superior graces, but because they feel that he will take their hands in a personal sense and walk with them the sacred path to their new adventure. No minister should give a blundering service nor render a clumsy ministry, but even worse would be for him to recite an impersonal and unfeeling ritual from which he kept himself apart. They want the minister, not just his services.

The minister must learn to share himself by learning how like he is to the people. He can learn from his own sorrowing the ways of reaching others who sorrow. He can learn from his own memory of guilt how best to preserve the integrity and dignity of a human life while condemning the sins committed.

Every sincere minister must glean from experiences with people a continually enlarging fund of knowledge in the area of practical, earthy living. Books cannot teach him the things that are demonstrated before his eyes by the people to whom he seeks to extend himself.

When a pastor goes with a delinquent boy through the rugged experiences of the courts and behind the cold walls of steel, he can learn much that will enrich his ministry to the continuing succession of delinquent boys whose lives he will touch. The minister must go into the divorce courts with his neighbors, observing the horrible miseries inflicted upon all, and thus continually enlarge his fund of knowledge and understanding. He must not only weep with those who weep but also learn firsthand about the sorrows of the human race, that he may the more ably serve those who day after day will look to him.

The life of the minister is that of a Christian person, and as such he may not personally experience the specific problems of those he seeks to help. For instance, he may not likely have had a personal problem with alcoholism, yet he must be able to help the alcoholic. He must eagerly learn from these associations what the real needs of people are. The minister who stands at the unique

THE MINISTER MUST READ BOOKS EXTENSIVELY, BUT HE MUST ALSO READ PEOPLE.

vantage point that is his beside the highway of life can accumulate a rich store of knowledge concerning human need. He can in one year watch, in his parish, life from the cradle to the grave. He can share in hundreds of lives at one time and glean collective truths from thousands of years of human experience. Other people experience births, marriages, and deaths only within their own family circles, while the minister gleans those experiences in a very personal and intimate manner from the entire community. He should be at once the best informed and the most experienced person of the community. He should always be on the alert to learn new truths, new techniques, new human needs, and new applications of the truth.

The minister must read books extensively, but he must also read people. He must know people and out of human suffering season his attitudes toward humankind. Many ministers watch others with a sort of detached curiosity without sufficient involvement to make possible their increased understanding. The minister who would enrich his ministry from his intimate exposures to others must be willing to take seriously the full responsibility that love levies upon him.

Sometimes clergy overlook the vast possibility for self-improvement that is often couched in their own experiences. If a minister is treated unkindly, he should learn more fully how painful unkindness is and guard his own words and acts more carefully. If he is misunderstood, the experience should help him to understand others. If he is neglected, a new awareness of the painfulness of neglect should result. If others are not cooperative, not dependable, not loyal, or not eager, the minister who suffers these frustrations should learn how important his own readiness to be cooperative and loyal. The minister whom another betrays should learn quickly never to cause another the pain of betrayal.

The true minister knows that he is expendable. He is of value as salt is valuable—giving flavor to that in which it loses itself. The minister must be prepared to share himself without complaint; for his success is not in personal accumulation but in the impact he can make upon others for the glory of God.

Jesus Christ counted not His life dear. He counted His debt to others ahead of His obligation to himself. He asked nothing of this earth and its men save a cross on which He might die and a borrowed tomb in which He might dress for Easter morning. What a surging joy came when on that Resurrection day men discovered that Jesus had found His life! They thought He had lost it! What an adventure He shared with the whole world by coming forth from the tomb triumphant!

No minister can know the abounding romance of living until his life is shared as Jesus shared. No minister can fully know the significance of finding life until he knows the adventure of losing it for the sake of those about him.

Not only his effectiveness but his fulfillment is determined by the amount of himself he shares. We become what we share as truly as we give what we share. The measure of the minister is not in training and skills alone but in the amount of these skills and graces that become available to others by reason of a close rapport and a vital proximity with people and with God.

Adapted from chapters 5 and 6 of *The Adventure of the Christian Ministry* (Kansas City: Beacon Hill Press of Kansas City, 1967), 49-68.

The pastor is important,

not because he is wiser

or better than are

other men, but because

he is so placed that

he may be able to draw out

and direct the powers

of other men.

—Elton Trueblood

From *The Incendiary Fellowship* (New York: Harper and Row, 1967), 36.

8

THREE QUALITIES GOD CAN USE TO INCREASE OUR EFFECTIVENESS

Raymond C. Kratzer

THE COMPONENT PARTS of a musical production are many and varied. It is difficult to assess what makes up a successful composition in terms of pleasure to the hearers. At times a seemingly perfect number will have little effect upon people, while another rather mediocre presentation will "ring the bell." That indescribable "something" is what makes the difference. Let's consider three of these "somethings," specific qualities God can use: holy recklessness, reverence, and forthrightness.

HOLY RECKLESSNESS

The success of a musical number, even on the modern scale, is to be able to throw oneself into the situation until there is a sense of soul impact that overrides the mere playing or singing of notes. The masters of traditional music get so "lost" in their performances that an indescribable ecstasy—an overtone—splashes onto the hearers.

Jeremiah one time decided to be a "proper preacher," just soft of reacting in a blasé manner. But the deterioration of his personality and the urgency of the hour got through to him. Here is what he said: "His word was in mine heart as a burning fire shut up in my bones, and I was weary with forbearing, and I could not stay" (Jer. 20:9).

The servant of God must refuse to be mechanical or unemotional in his work. If he moves people, he must be moved. If others are to be stirred to action, there must be a holy ferment in the pastor's own soul. In reality, when the preacher thinks about the possibilities of ministry, he cannot help getting excited about it. Ps. 39:3 gives a graphic picture of the metamorphosis of reflective thinking in the Christian perspective: "My heart was hot within me, while I was musing the fire burned: THEN SPAKE I WITH MY TONGUE."

Someone has said, "We need more tears in our religion and in our ministry." Perhaps if issues tore at our hearts sufficiently, we would have tears of compassion as we went about our ministry.

On the other hand, a "holy recklessness" does not imply a thoughtless abandon of the emotions. Rather it is a planned attack on lethargy, on mediocrity, and on deadly formalism. I have seen preachers who got so carried away on some religious hobby that their excitement caused them to say unwise and irrelevant things. Their seeming zeal lacked knowledge and harmed rather than helped the cause. Their presentation was "like sounding brass and a tinkling cymbal."

Some ministers have exuded a moving spirit when they expounded truth, although their volume did not approximate a cyclone. Theirs was the dynamic of an electrical charge born of the unction of God on their soul, together with the intensity of the truth that gripped them. I recall vividly a dear old preacher who was unable to stand throughout his sermon because of failing strength. But his Spirit-anointed message, well formulated and poured forth from a burning heart, moved the entire congregation.

May God help us to move from a matter-of-fact type of ministry to a do-or-die spirit. The urgency of the hour demands a "touch of eternity" in our approach to the work of the Lord. We are evangels of the Most High God in whom has been entrusted the message of reconciliation. The acceptance of our message may mean the salvation or the damnation of those we come in contact with. As Jude puts it: "And some . . . making a difference . . . pulling them out of the fire" (Jude 22-23).

> **DON'T BE AFRAID TO SET SOME AMBITIOUS GOALS AND THEN GO OUT TO REACH THEM.**

When we go all out for God, refusing to be licked by momentary setbacks, the Holy Spirit will infuse us with new life, help us to develop challenging plans, and thrill us with amazing progress. Barren altars, diminishing attendance, and losing statistics will be reversed.

Don't be afraid to set some ambitious goals and then go out to reach them. How about one new family per month won to the Lord and added to your church? Spend enough time in prayer for God to bathe your soul with compassion. Study your strategy thoroughly enough until your "web of concern" will be placed expertly about the object of your plans. Involve all the help you may need in prayer warriors, planned visits, and personal evangelism. Don't let your time-goal slip by without coming to grips with a direct, compassionate appeal to those you have set out to win. You may be surprised how God will hook onto your efforts and prepare the prospect for the final surrender—to Him. Remember in your strategy that you are out to save a lost soul and bring him to Christ—not necessarily to the church. Instead of the approach: "I wish you would come to my church," it should be: "I wish you would become acquainted with my Christ—He's the answer to all of our needs."

Revivals are so often ineffective because of too little holy recklessness in their plans. One pastor said: "I didn't get any advertising out for this meeting because people don't read it anyway." Result: a small, weak revival. Others often expect a designated time, a good evangelist, and a comfortable church building to do the job. These all help, but little will be done unless better plans are laid.

The most effective meeting results from the best of preparation. It would be worth a try to organize prayer groups many weeks before a planned revival. Then a class for Christian workers could be trained in dealing with people at an altar. Likewise, these persons could be instructed to sit in strategic places throughout the church, near to where potential seekers sit. When the altar call was being made, they could be available to inconspicuously speak to needy souls by whom they are standing, offering to accompany them to the altar. They could likewise be alerted to go immediately to the altar with anyone who might step forward to pray with them.

Oh, what a symphony could be produced if . . . if . . . if our pastors and people would but tune the instruments of their sanctified personalities to reverberate the overtone of compassion, born of a holy recklessness. Oh, let us become red-hot for God and see the tide turn in our Zion.

HOLY REVERENCE

From the earliest pages of sacred writ to the last chronicler of God's Word, there is a constant, haunting overtone of reverence and awe concerning sacred things. Moses was asked to remove his shoes as he stood at the sacred ground of God's will for his life while standing before the burning bush. Isaiah was entranced by the cherubim and seraphim repeating, "Holy, Holy, Holy is the Lord," when he entered the sanctuary of the Most High. Peter, James, and John were overcome by the effulgent glory surrounding Jesus as they shared with Him the Transfiguration experience.

We find ourselves at times caught up in the mood of the day, which considers nothing sacred. Morality, leadership, institutionalism, the government, the school, and even the church are charaded by well-paid entertainers who seem to please the populace. The appellations of "Superstar" and the "Man upstairs" to our blessed Redeemer are carelessly mouthed by unregenerate persons and often condoned in substance by the silent majority.

> STRIVE WITH EVERY AVAILABLE TOOL TO RECAPTURE TRADITIONAL REVERENCE CONCERNING SACRED THINGS.

The ministry must strive with every available tool to recapture traditional reverence concerning sacred things, lest our current generation lose completely the basic foundations upon which a God-pleasing life can be built.

The dramatic and terrifying experiences outlined in the Bible of persons who flippantly handled sacred things, or who carelessly regarded God's instructions, must be considered as "teachers" to guide us in this day of grace. The misappropriation of the spoils at Jericho in the case of Achan at Ai caused terrible judgment to come to him and his family. Uzza, who put forth his hand and touched the ark of the covenant to steady it when the oxen stumbled who were hauling it, was smitten dead by the hand of God because he disregarded the importance of sacred things. Ananias and Sapphira died in an instant because they lied concerning their gifts to the church. And because God's judgments today are not so immediate is no sign that impiety is less grievous to Him or will receive less punishment in the long run.

Too often good preachers will relate a story to gain a laugh in which sacred things are put in a frivolous light. Repetition in this vein will dull the conscience of the servant of God, and it will also damage the image of reverence that should always be a part of his life. Even the way he laughs at the impiety of others can "ring a bell" of uncertainty or shallowness.

The attitude of the minister toward his church—even the church building itself—can enhance the image of reverence that must be recaptured in this day of such irreverence. Just recently a dedicated layman of our Zion met me at one of our small churches. Since he was a real estate man, I had asked him to appraise the building prior to our advertising it for sale. The day was cold and the interior of the church seemed even colder. I walked ahead of him into the sanctuary with my hat on to protect my head. But as he walked through the door, without fanfare, he almost automatically doffed his hat and held it in his hand as he looked the church over. Of course I followed suit. My heart was warmed that day—even if my head was cool—because of the aura of reverence that pervaded the atmosphere.

Little things speak loudly at times. The manner in which the pastor holds his Bible and the skill with which he reads it can sound forth a sweet tone of reverence. The public prayer, indicating that the man or woman of God goes to the holy place of prayer often, can stimulate a whole congregation to experience the presence of God. The way he places his offering in the plate as the firstfruits of his labors can lift the offering to a place of sacramental glory.

We would not at all try to say that the pastor is to enshrine a sanctimonious robot by his performances. No one should more fully epitomize the joy of the Lord by his whole life than the minister. He should evoke the heartiest of laughter and the most exciting type of living. But he should always remember there is a "time and a season for every thing under the sun." But there is never a time for him to deviate from his influential position so as to make his shibboleths sound like "clanging cymbals and tinkling bells."

It is strange that at times holiness people are fearful of appearing prudish or "holier than thou" to their fellows. This compulsion causes some ministers to inhibit their finer motives and exhibit a false joviality that causes heartaches and a throbbing conscience at the end of the day. After all, what is wrong in being thought of as "the man or woman of God"? Could it be that our carelessness along this line prevents the full blessing of God moving in our midst many times?

Through thoughtful and daily discipline, one's life can speak volumes that will extend and broaden the scope of pastoral usefulness. History is full of illustrations of preachers who changed their world for good because they dared to be different. I can recall many across the years who caused me to feel that God was speaking through them, because they possessed an attitude of awe for the holy. Their messages had a touch of eternity in them, and people were changed for the better because they came in contact with them.

Let us as ministers dare to be different, not being conformed to this world, but rather exuding the transformation that we preach as the possibility of divine grace. Aping the styles, accommodating to the flairs of society can only place us on a lower plane, which will increase the difficulty of the task of lifting others to the higher life. Let us align ourselves to God's pattern and strive to produce the kind of influence God can use.

THROUGH THOUGHTFUL AND DAILY DISCIPLINE, ONE'S LIFE CAN SPEAK VOLUMES THAT WILL EXTEND AND BROADEN THE SCOPE OF PASTORAL USEFULNESS.

HOLY FORTHRIGHTNESS

The genius of a sanctified life is a crystal-clear transparency of character that allows for no shadows to distort a heart made perfect in love. It results in an open countenance in which there is no deceit or uncertainty where truth is concerned. A straightforwardness of manner is manifested by a lilting voice and a positive attitude, born of a heart cleansed from all sin.

Daniel is such a great example. You recall that after he had been chief of the presidents of the realm of Darius, jealousy caused the other princes to connive to destroy him. He had been chosen for this place of leadership because the king observed an excellent spirit in him. Likewise, his enemies could find no fault or error in him, but only faithfulness to his task. And even when they planned his destruction through the foolish decree the king was enticed to sign, he never deviated from his standards of life. In due season it won for him the victory.

In the ministry there are few things more despicable than a preacher who is uncertain in the area of his beliefs and standards. I recall a certain pastor of a large denomination who said quite frankly that he didn't know whether he was saved or not, and that he doubted whether this were possible to know at all.

The New Testament is replete with positive affirmations about truth. Jesus said, "I am the Way, the Truth, and the Life." Paul said, "I know whom I have believed, and am persuaded that He is able to keep that which I have committed unto Him against that day."

We need a clarion sound to our ministry that will cause people to know where we stand as far as doctrine and standards are concerned. As God's servants we should unashamedly proclaim the Apostles' Creed as set forth by our forebears. We should forthrightly declare our Agreed Statement of Belief in

One God—the Father, Son, and Holy Spirit. That the Old and New Testament Scriptures, given by plenary inspiration, contain all truth necessary to faith and Christian living. That man is born with a fallen nature, and is therefore, inclined to evil, and that continually. That the finally impenitent are hopelessly and eternally lost. That the atonement through Jesus Christ is for the whole human race; and that whosoever repents and believes on the Lord Jesus Christ is justified and regenerated and saved from the dominion of sin. That believers are to be sanctified wholly, subsequent to regeneration, through faith in the Lord Jesus Christ. That the Holy Spirit bears witness to the new birth, and also to the entire sanctification of believers. That our Lord will return, the dead will be raised, and the final judgment will take place (*Manual*).

People may not agree with us, but they can know that we are convinced of our beliefs. Our message must ring true and must echo the God-inspired doctrines that have given our church its birth and its remarkable growth and development.

In order to produce tones of music, the strings of a violin must be stretched between two poles until some pressure is exerted on them. If they hang loose, they will emit only a dull, flapping sound. But when connected to the tailpiece in the lower end of the instrument, and to the tuning pins on the upper neck of the instrument and drawn tight, their overtones become delightful when controlled by the musician. Likewise, when we connect our faith to the eternal God above us, and fasten it securely in the depths of our nature, allowing God to remove all of the slack by His skilled hand, then an overtone of victory will be the order of the day.

TRUTH IS POWERFUL WHEN DECLARED BY ONE WHOSE INNER NATURE REFLECTS THE TRUTH.

The forthrightness of Jesus left His interrogators speechless. Truth is powerful when declared by one whose inner nature reflects the truth. That is why the message of holiness, proclaimed through holy lips, makes such an impact.

Let us examine our inner life to be sure there is no slack in our commitment or in our message. Paul could say, "Follow me as I follow the Lord," because no one could contradict his message on the basis of his conduct. He lived what he preached.

There are times in the life of the minister when he is called upon to demonstrate the validity of his preaching. He has heralded forth a gospel that purports to hold one steady when the storm is on, and enables one to return good for evil and love for hate. But when he has been ill-used, it is so easy to return kind for kind. Someone said: "It is manly to resent it, but it is godly to forgive it." The minister must always react from the stance of his high calling.

A pastor was ill in the hospital one time. The nurses decided to give him the works to see if his performance matched his oratory. They did everything to irritate him including being slow to answer his buzzer as well as other exasperating incidents. But he came through. He manifested patience and kindness and refused to scold or berate them for their apparent neglect. The truth of the matter is that the minister is on trial all of the time, whether or not planned for. Consequently, he needs to keep his soul in tune and refuse to allow an "off-key" note to sound forth from situations in his life, whether in the church, the home, the shop, on the telephone, or any other situation.

In the words of Jesus, we should "let [our] light so shine before men, that they may see [our] good works, and glorify [our] Father which is in heaven" (Matt. 5:16).

From a monthly newsletter to pastors on the Northwest District, something like "Paul writing to Timothy."

Leadership is earned
and not conferred.
You may be well trained,
ordained, and assigned
or elected
to a significant position
in a church,
but you are not
a leader until some group
believes in you enough
to follow you.

—Dale Galloway

From *Leading in Times of Change* (Kansas City: Beacon Hill Press of Kansas City, 2001), 35.

9

WHAT ACHIEVEMENT DOES GOD EXPECT FROM US?

Neil B. Wiseman

"BLOOM BUSTERS helped me grow these flowers, the greatest gardening success I've ever had," the shopkeeper in Red Stone, Colorado, said in response to my comments about her flowers. She had the most extraordinary red geraniums I had ever seen. Garden catalog illustrations seem inferior by comparison.

At the first sign of spring, you can be sure I started shopping for Bloom Busters. I found several plant foods with similar names, but I never located Bloom Busters.

The shopkeeper might have misspoken. Maybe I misunderstood, or perhaps I did not shop in the right stores. But if Bloom Busters does not exist, some entrepreneur should market a plant food by that name.

That name started me thinking about frontline pastors I know. They do everything they can to be a vessel for God in a hurting world. They work and pray and struggle. Yet, in spite of their sacrificial commitments and demanding schedules, their churches often grow only slightly or shrink a little every year. Like working in a wilting garden in a scorching August sun, their sizable efforts never break growth barriers. Nothing unusual happens in their congregations. They feel like the tired old preacher who said, "My necessities ate up my possibilities." They starve for the reality they lost when ministry was allowed to become secularized, professionalized, miniaturized, and marginalized. They hunger for a new grip on ministry.

They seek a fresh anointing and a new perspective. They want something to happen inside them similar to the 40-year-old pastor who reported after serving his rural Georgia church for 10 years, "When I allowed myself to be fascinated by opportunities and by the grace of God, I started blooming in ways I never experienced before."

New ministry blooming in familiar places requires that we take a discriminating look at existing ministry activities even as we carefully scrutinize our opportunities. Most settings have extraordinary possibilities that no one may envision on the surface. For example, outreach makes ministry grow faster than administrative activities do, and marriage workshops usually are more effective than divorce restoration counseling.

A beginning New England pastor wrote to me, saying, "I don't have time for outreach because I am too busy studying for next Sunday's sermon, stomping out brushfires, and trying to meet the unrealistic demands of people in the church."

Could it be that more emphasis on outreach would change the focus of his ministry and would challenge the perceptions of the members of his small church? Making such a shift would be tough, but it is the only way new opportunities for his church will be set in motion.

Larger Blooms and Lasting Fruit

One reality is obvious: God wants every ministry to bloom, to bear magnificent fruit, and to have strong roots. He wants His people fed and loved in every place. He does not, however, expect each pastor to look alike, to grow at the same rate, or to have the same impact. That is why He planted you where you are.

Several key challenges must be faced if ministry in a specific place is to be renewed, reenergized, or even revolutionized. Try scoring yourself on this checklist:

- Am I willing and able to revitalize and to restate my ministry so it attracts contemporary people and kindles excitement for the others?
- Can I take the life-changing force of the gospel to the cutting edges of life where the substitutes for faith have proven trivial and futile?
- Can I help secular people see the gospel as an appealing alternative to the security, sex, fame, and power they chase?
- Can one pastor change the world?
- Can my ministry thrive in a tough place where effective ministry has never occurred?
- What did God have in mind for me to accomplish in this place when He called me here?

Everyone knows that flourishing gardens need quality seed, cultivating, watering, weeding, meticulous attention to soil conditions and temperature. But my Red Stone gardener friend multiplied her success and satisfaction when she added generous amounts of tender loving care and nourishing plant food.

Ministry is like that—tender loving care and bloom busters must be added to grow spiritually vibrant congregations. After years of developing believers in my own churches and observing hundreds of pastors at work, I believe these bloom busters will make ministry flourish and will enable pastors to bloom where God has planted them.

Try them for yourself. I guarantee you that the people you serve will remember more about the person you are than about the words you say.

MEASURE POTENTIAL GOD'S WAY

I loved the way one church described itself in an advertisement seeking a new pastor: "A DIAMOND IN THE ROUGH is searching for a master stonecutter to unleash the potential that lies beneath its surface. This GEM TO BE can be found in a suburban neighborhood in South-Central Pennsylvania. . . . If you have a steady hand, keen eye, and are willing to 'strike the blow' to produce dazzling results, write to . . ."[1] Maybe every church is a diamond in the rough, waiting for a master stonecutter to strike the blow to unleash its potential.

View Your Church as a Living Cell

Take another careful look at your diamond in the rough.

In *Diary of a Country Priest,* Georges Bernanos writes tenderly about his congregation: "This morning I prayed hard for my parish, my poor parish, my first and perhaps my last, since I ask no better than to die here. My parish! The words can't even be spoken without a kind of soaring love. . . . I know that my parish is a reality; it is not a mere administrative segment, but a living cell of the everlasting Church."[2]

It is nearly impossible for a pastor to see his church as a living cell of the everlasting Church when he is bogged down with the confusing expectations of dear old Sister Smith or while he is dealing with the sad sorrow of a dying teenager. This is probably the reason pastors usually see more problems than possibilities in the place where the Father has planted them. The inability to see the forest because we are in the midst of the trees certainly applies.

Can you see it clearly and believe it thoroughly? Your church is a living cell of the everlasting Church.

Play Prospective Pastor

To reevaluate your opportunities, try playing prospective pastor for a full day once or twice each year. Drive or walk through your surroundings as if you were seeing the setting for the first time. Refocus on the potential you saw when you first visited this place.

Dare to dream your original dream again. See your congregation as live, flesh-and-blood people—some noble and some neurotic, some saintly and some sinful, some great and some not so great. The routines you feel and experience day after day or year after year may become brand-new. Remember, God intends for ministry to thrive everywhere people reside.

Recently, a bored young pastor phoned to ask, "What comes next after pastoring?" He continued, "I've been thinking about trying teaching or law or social work." What comes next? His question implies he does not measure potential in his church the way God does.

"GOD, SHOW ME WHAT YOU WANT DONE IN THIS PART OF YOUR HARVEST."

All things considered, who could be satisfied with the narrower spiritual opportunities other occupations offer when a person could be a pastor? The possibilities are enormous and eternal. To see them clearly, every parish minister needs to pray often, "God, show me what You want done in this part of Your harvest."

Opportunity blindness always worsens when a pastor considers each assignment as a stepping-stone to something better. Such a stance forces him to consider every pastorate as semitemporary and in some unexplainable, self-fulfilling way, his thinking causes the assignment to actually become restrictive and suffocating and enslaving. Without his realizing it, opportunities he hopes to find in another place often already exist where he resides.

Francis Bacon's advice helps us bloom: "A wise man makes more opportunities than he finds."[3] I would imagine that any long-term pastor has considered moving to another place only to be reminded by the Lord, "I have not released you; I need you here; your work is not finished."

Marking Time Costs Too Much

The human cost of marking time, while waiting for something better, can be frighteningly high. Those we could have won for Christ continue in their sinful alienation. Broken homes we could have mended go to the divorce courts. Innocent children we could have introduced to the Savior move on to adulthood without hearing the name of Jesus. Church members atrophy. Our passion for service shrivels.

Multiply these losses across a few thousand congregations and it adds up to alarming spiritual barrenness for a country and a culture. As we move deeper into the 21st century, the issue of apathy may be our number one problem. Possibilities are clouded when a pastor feels overwhelmed by the massive and compelling spiritual needs he sees around him everywhere. As a result, sin and secularism are devastatingly oppressive to him.

But consider the presuppositions of ministry again. Doesn't a call to ministry mean that God may send a pastor to wretched situations He wants to redeem and to people He wants to save? Doesn't ministry mean that God sends us, inadequate though we are, next door to hell to make the setting more like heaven? He has to have *someone* there as His agent of reconciliation.

A pastor yearning for an easy assignment is as strange as a missionary wanting to go to an overevangelized nation instead of a place where people have never heard about Christ.

Consider Two Perspectives from Jesus

Jesus viewed potential from two perspectives: while using a towel to wash dirty feet, and from the Cross.

God usually assigns us to a place where we are most needed, even when we long for an easier place. God may need us in a tough place where the salary is low and the housing is limited. Perhaps He will assign us to places of urban decay, social violence, or moral desperation. Maybe He will send us to congregations splintered by broken relationships. He might want us to serve brutal, greedy, exploitative people because we are their only hope.

Perhaps God intends for us to feed faith and love to people in places where they have given up and who may also be suspicious and hostile. Let's face it, pastors throughout the long, stirring march of Christian history have often bloomed best in moral barnyards. When a pastor begins to evaluate potential from Jesus' perspective, every congregation possesses extraordinary possibilities. Every church and community then seems ready for a spiritual awakening. Of course, incredibly difficult assignments force a pastor to absolute dependence on God. Why be terrified or intimidated? We are linked in strength-giving partnership with omnipotence.

GOD MAY NEED US IN A TOUGH PLACE WHERE THE SALARY IS LOW AND THE HOUSING IS LIMITED.

Create an Ideal Assignment

Maybe every minister dreams of a perfect pastorate—whatever that is. Many expect to be surprised by some ministerial fantasy around the next bend. Others hope their ideal will show up before Christmas.

Some people spend their entire ministry in search of a model congregation made up of hundreds of good-natured people in a moderate climate, in an ideal town, with high pay. Still others fret for years, coveting a task God never grants them. For many, it's wanting what another pastor has without considering the problems that go with it.

Apparently the pastors who long for greener pastures have never considered the reality that every good place once required someone to transform a tough assignment into a special, desirable church by blooming there. Such an idealized assignment may be similar to beauty in the eye of the beholder.

Ideal for someone will be a country congregation or a city storefront, a church planted in a new development or a 100-year-old congregation, or maybe a home Bible study group or a congregation of 500 or 5,000. The secret is to make your assignment ideal by blooming where God plants you.

Expanding our views of potential even more, a young pastor suggests wisdom beyond his years, "I do not think a minister should move until he has experienced a spiritual breakthrough where he is."

Careful, there is a surprising bear trap in his concept. He continues, "Who would ever want to leave a place while an authentic spiritual breakthrough is taking place?" This view helps us see incredible possibilities in every setting and undermines the human frustration and financial costs of moving to another church. An absolutely indispensable factor in sustaining a healthy ministry is the willingness to view one's setting from God's perspective.

A church leader in Canada suggests, "Every church has a right to have a pastor who believes something spiritually significant will happen in that place under his leadership. If a pastor does not believe in the possibilities of his assignment, he should seek God until he sees potentiality." More than mere strategy, this is the pastoral leadership tree trunk out of which branches of effective ministry grow.

God counts on you to achieve a miraculous ministry in the place where He has planted you. He has no one else to fill your place. Growing a magnificent ministry in any location can be started or renewed by finding a need that breaks your heart and then breaking your back to meet that need.

FIND FULFILLMENT WHERE YOU ARE

A NAGGING QUEST FOR MEANING IS A UNIVERSAL HUMAN HUNGER.

A yearning to be whole, to make one's life count, and to make a difference in the world are what makes a potential pastor open to God's call into ministry. A nagging quest for meaning is a universal human hunger. Most of the world continues looking for the prize in the wrong places. But ministry majors on meaning.

A pastor on Florida's Gold Coast was called to a 100-member church made up of mostly elderly people. He followed a pastor who had served this congregation for more than 20 years. He had been there so long that few people in the congregation could remember the former pastor. To complicate matters, many members of the congregation lived across the street from the church in a Social Security supplement high-rise building. As a result, the new pastor faced unusually heavy demands for pastoral care. Some of his minister friends warned him that the situation was futile, but he saw beyond the limitations.

In eight years, the new pastor started Bible studies in the high-rise facility, recruited immigrants from Haiti, Cuba, Mexico, and Finland to start six language churches, began a youth ministry, purchased five nearby houses for sanctuary expansion, and offered genuine friendship to the former pastor who lived nearby.

The new minister saw beyond age, color, language, and limitation. After he had been there for several years, one of his friends who had advised him not to accept the pastorate offered this compliment: "You took lemons and made lemonade."

During an interview for a pastor's magazine in which he was asked about finding ministry fulfillment in tough assignments, this minister responded: "Complain about difficulties? Emphasize hardships? Bellyache about inconvenience? Many do and so could I. But what's the point? There's so much more to ministry. I choose to hope, explore, cherish, contribute, and live. I enjoy seeing how much fun I can have in the ministry."

This minister's ability to find meaning, fulfillment, and satisfaction were natural results of a long succession of doing the right things for the right reasons across years of cheerful, Christ-centered service.

THE SERENDIPITY OF SELFLESS SERVICE IS ABIDING SATISFACTION.

His formula for fulfillment: Expect every assignment to enrich your life and it will not disappoint you. The serendipity of selfless service is abiding satisfaction. Loving gives us love. Serving supplies satisfaction. Giving oneself away enriches us.

How to Increase Fulfillment

To increase satisfaction, rekindle your original motivations for ministry. Rejoice in your achievements. Celebrate your victories as God-given enablements that flow into the nooks and cubbyholes of your ministry.

Tame your workaholic tendencies so you can find time to grow a great soul. Read old and new books about ministry to establish a benchmark for your pastoral service. Find successful models to emulate. Doing these ecclesiastical calisthenics on a regular basis prevents spiritual stagnation, professional passivity, and superficial success.

Let's admit that every pastor stands at the center of what makes ministry meaningful. The springs of fulfillment are internal and personal. The whole thing starts with that first stirring in your soul about ministry; no one else heard the dialogue and debate between you and God. Because God called you, it means you measure fulfillment differently from people in other occupations or other pastors. It means you are fulfilled when God is most pleased with your ministry.

Fulfillment Is an Inside Job

Unless ministers find a high level of meaning in their work, they almost never significantly impact a congregation or a community. Take an example from army history: A subordinate on General George C. Marshall's staff during World War II reported that several officers were having low morale problems.

General Marshall retorted, "Officers don't have morale problems. Officers cure morale problems in themselves and others. No one looks after my morale."[4] He is probably right about military personnel, and he certainly says a lot to ministers. No pastor can depend on anyone else feeding his feelings of fulfillment. It is an inside job, but anyone can achieve it.

A pastor in a mid-Atlantic state, let's call him Tom, has served a series of congregations for 31 years. He is confused about when to expect his satisfactions. To a trusted friend, he spoke sadly: "All my life, I followed scripts suggested by my parents, wife, church members, and even my bishop. And when their scripts conflicted, I just tried harder. But I haven't experienced much fulfillment. I've done

GENUINE FULFILLMENT IS ROOTED IN KNOWING WHAT MINISTRY IS AND IN DOING IT.

my duty, but it hasn't been too much fun. My life is melancholy and drab." Now, at age 55, Tom keeps waiting for someone to give him his fulfillment, but he fears it will never come. And he's probably right.

How tragic! Tom should have awakened years ago to the fact that no outside circumstance or person provides meaning for a pastor. Fate does not assign anyone the task of making ministry meaningful for us.

Genuine fulfillment is rooted in knowing what ministry is and in doing it energetically and creatively. Better than anyone else, you know when your ministry is vibrant and satisfying. You know what pleases God. This is what matters most in measuring meaning in ministry.

Fulfillment Is an Intentional Choice

Unfortunately, a pastor never gains an ounce of fulfillment by saying, "I know I should build a satisfying ministry, but I don't get the breaks or have the luck or possess natural abilities." Far better to realize that every minister can have more meaning if and when he wants it.

Admittedly, finding fulfillment takes more work in some places than in others. But take heart! Pastor Ron Mehl of the Beaverton (Oregon) Foursquare Church explains the fountainhead of fulfillment, "God sees the fine, strong character qualities we will develop in the future while we see ourselves muddling through perplexity and setbacks and sudden reversals."[5] Many gospel harvest hands believe hardships produce the sweetest satisfactions.

One writer suggests that discovering fulfillment is like experiencing a hot stove. After touching a blistering flame, one can draw back forever and announce, "I will never touch a stove again."

A different reaction is more desirable. One can turn down the heat, follow the instruction book, have the stove repaired, and become a gourmet cook. Then the cook has the satisfaction of serving a superb meal and many are well-fed. In a similar way, pastors can either quit or find ways to increase their influence for God.

A warning must be considered. Most pastors easily discern God's fulfillment in their yesterdays, but they struggle about today. Why not watch carefully for God in your present moments instead of working so hard to sharpen your 20/20 hindsight? Why not turn today's troublesome circumstances into magnificent fulfillment? Spectacular blooming often depends on how we choose.

UNDERSTAND YOUR IMPORTANCE

God needs you now more than ever. The human race cannot afford to lose one more committed pastor. Without the salt of your ministry, society could putrefy. Without your light, the darkness could grow blacker still.

Although these current days confuse us, we may be the only hope for faith, righteousness, and truth to be rechiseled into society's psyche. We must recognize how much our troubled world needs us.

A miraculous spiritual revolution is needed to clean up the immoral cesspool that is drowning us. We must intercede for an awakening. We must speak of the gospel again with a supernatural anointing. This cannot be accomplished by ministers who give up a day too soon, by those who suffer from professional inferiority complexes or by those who turn and run at the first sign of formidable opposition. Who will give our neighbors God's good news about forgiveness and grace and reconciliation if we don't? This is what God trusts us to do for our drifting society.

A MIRACULOUS SPIRITUAL REVOLUTION IS NEEDED TO CLEAN UP THE IMMORAL CESSPOOL THAT IS DROWNING US.

The power to alleviate this darkness is in our hearts and in our hands. We can light the lamps, stay the course, and stop cursing the darkness. The fact that the world needs us so urgently makes it possible for us to bloom in lots of dark places.

Here's how. Define ministry accurately and clearly. Sharpen your perspective through Scripture, church history, believers, and fellow ministers. Know what the target is. Check the promises again. Then, intentionally implement Christ's mandate in your ministry. And challenge the enemy with your whole-hearted commitment to Christ.

1. *Monday Morning* (Louisville, Ky.: General Assembly Council of the Presbyterian Church, USA, 1993), 45.

2. Georges Bernanos, *Diary of a Country Priest* (New York: Carroll and Graf Publishers, 1937), 28.

3. Francis Bacon, *A Strategy for Daily Living* (New York: Free Press, 1973), 22.

4. John W. Gardner, *On Leadership* (New York: Free Press, 1990), 198.

5. Ron Mehl, *Surprise Endings* (Sisters, Oreg.: Multnomah Books, 1993), 172.

CONTRIBUTORS TO
A HOLY CALLING

MILO L. ARNOLD

Rev. Milo L. Arnold was a model pastor who multiplied his influential ministry beyond the local congregation through radio and publishing. He served the church for 38 years as pastor, mostly in the northwest areas of North America. In 1968, he became the first professor of practical theology at the newly formed Nazarene Bible College at Colorado Springs. His ministry of publishing included *Parents Can Be a Problem, The Christian Adventure, Excuses Answered, This Adventure Called Marriage,* and *This Adventure Called Ministry.*

JOHN C. BOWLING

Dr. John C. Bowling, president of Olivet Nazarene University, is the author of over 60 articles and three books: *A Way with Words, Grace-Full Leadership,* and *Packin' Up and Headin' Out.* He taught on the faculties of Nazarene Bible College and Olivet Nazarene University in the 1970s, and then moved on to pastoring, first at Dallas First Church of the Nazarene and then at Kankakee College Church. Dr. Bowling served in that pastorate until 1991, when he was elected president of ONU.

RAYMOND C. KRATZER

Dr. Raymond C. Kratzer began his ministry as a pastor in Arlington, Oregon, in 1938. He continued pastoral service in Oregon and Idaho until 1960 when he was elected district superintendent of the Northwest District. After 19 years of service as district superintendent, he has served many churches on the Northwest District as interim pastor during retirement. The material published in chapter 8 of this book comes from his monthly pastoral development letter series, a kind of "Paul to Timothy" approach that he sent every month to the ministry team on the Northwest District.

JANINE T. METCALF

Dr. Janine Metcalf left a successful career as a television news anchor in Southern California to join the pastoral staff of Pasadena First Church in 1984, where she served as pastor to senior adults for seven years. Her testimony of her conversion while covering the Iranian hostage crisis is well-known in Nazarene circles. The journey to her current pastorate in El Cajon, California, has included service as an evangelist and retreat speaker, professor at Point Loma Nazarene University and Nazarene Theological Seminary, coauthor of *The Upward Call: Spiritual Formation and the Holy Life,* and most recently, producer of the video documentary *Ablaze with Love: The Living Legacy of Our Nazarene Foremothers.*

JERRY D. PORTER

Dr. Jerry D. Porter was elected the 31st general superintendent in 1997, while serving as district superintendent of the Washington (D.C.) District. Previous to his assignment in Washington, he served as director of the Mexico-Central America Region from 1986 to 1992. Earlier, Porter served as rector of the Nazarene Seminary of the Americas in Costa Rica before his appointment as regional director. Except for two years in the pastorate at Angleton, Texas, all his previous service to Christ and the church was as a missionary on the MAC Region. He and his wife, Toni, started their ministry as church-planting missionaries to the Dominican Republic in 1975.

EUGENE L. STOWE

Dr. Eugene L. Stowe began his ministry in 1944 in Visalia, California. From there he went on to give pastoral leadership to Nazarene congregations in Oakland, California; Salem, Oregon; and Nampa, Idaho. He was elected district superintendent of the newly formed Central California District in 1963. Before completing his first four-year term as district superintendent, Stowe was elected president of Nazarene Theological Seminary and two years later, in 1968, was elected general superintendent. Previous to his election as general superintendent, he served on the general board and the General NYPS Council. He authored two books: *The Spiritual Glow* and *The Ministry of Shepherding.* Dr. Stowe was the visionary who founded the first PALCON.

R. T. WILLIAMS

Dr. R. T. Williams, at age 25, united with the people called Nazarenes and was ordained by Dr. P. F. Bresee at the 1908 general assembly. Between 1908 and 1916, he served in several ministry roles as pastor of Nashville First Church, church-planting evangelist, professor and president of Peniel University. In 1916, Williams was elected general superintendent and served until 1946. Among the second wave of leaders in the new denomination, Dr. Williams became one of the most influential leaders in the formative days of the young denomination. His book *Pastor and People,* the first pastoral ministry book, helped define and shape the role of the pastor in the church.

G. B. WILLIAMSON

Dr. G. B. Williamson pastored 16 years in Farmington, Iowa; Chicago; and Cleveland before being elected president of Eastern Nazarene College in 1936. He served there until 1945, when he was called to pastor Kansas City First Church of the Nazarene. The next year, Dr. Williamson was elected general superintendent, a position he held for 23 years. In 1968, at age 70, at a time when most people retire, Dr. and Mrs. Williamson joined the faculty of Nazarene Bible College, Colorado Springs, where they both taught for nearly 10 years. Williamson, more than any other one individual, challenged the church to establish the Bible college. His wide-ranging ministry extended to writing as well; he authored eight books, including *Overseers of the Flock, Preaching Scriptural Holiness,* and biographies of Roy T. Williams and R. C. Ingram.

NEIL B. WISEMAN

Dr. Neil B. Wiseman had pastorates in California, Washington, Colorado, and Florida. He has served in education at Trevecca Nazarene University (6 years) and Nazarene Bible College (15 years). He holds degrees from Olivet Nazarene University, Nazarene Theological Seminary, and Vanderbilt Divinity School. His service to the denomination includes director of PALCON I, founding editor of *GROW* magazine, director of Small Church Institute, and editor of *Preacher's Magazine,* producer of the Layman's Tape Club and the Minister's Tape Club and the first editor of the Dialog Series. He has written and/or edited 20 books.